John Corbett

The Lake Country

An Annal of olden Days in Central New York - The Land of Gold

John Corbett

The Lake Country
An Annal of olden Days in Central New York - The Land of Gold

ISBN/EAN: 9783337237639

Printed in Europe, USA, Canada, Australia, Japan

Cover: Foto ©ninafisch / pixelio.de

More available books at **www.hansebooks.com**

THE LAKE COUNTRY.

AN ANNAL OF OLDEN DAYS IN CENTRAL NEW YORK.

THE LAND OF GOLD.

BY
JOHN CORBETT.

ROCHESTER, N. Y.
DEMOCRAT AND CHRONICLE PRINT,
1898.

THE TOPICS.

TITLE.	PAGE.
THE LAKES	8
THE IROQUOIS	11
THE EXPEDITION	13
THE INVASION	16
THE ENGAGEMENT	19
THE DEVASTATION	21
THE ENCAMPMENTS	24
THE BARBARITIES	27
THE RETREAT	30
THE CHRONICLE	33
THE TRADITIONS	36
THE COMMANDERS	39
THE SACHEMS	42
THE WOMEN	44
THE TREATIES	47
THE PRE-EMPTION	50
THE TITLES	53
THE ESTATES	56
THE COUNTIES	58
THE OFFICIALS	62
THE PIONEERS	65
THE SETTLEMENT	68
THE DEVELOPMENT	71
THE INDUSTRIES	73
THE ANTIQUITIES	76
THE LANDMARKS	79
THE TRAVELERS	82
THE MILITIA	85

THE TOPICS.

TITLE.	PAGE
The Schools	88
The Institutions	91
The Religion	93
The Folk-lore	96
The Treasure	99
The Salt-springs	102
The Rocks	105
The Streams	108
The Waterways	110
The Steamboats	113
The Ferries	116
The Canals	119
The Land-routes	122
The Stage-lines	125
The Railways	128
The Press	130
The Sloops	133
The Fruits	136

THE SKETCHES.

The Ship	144
The Camp	147
The Claim	149
The Gold	151
The Scene	154
The Shore	156
The Race	159

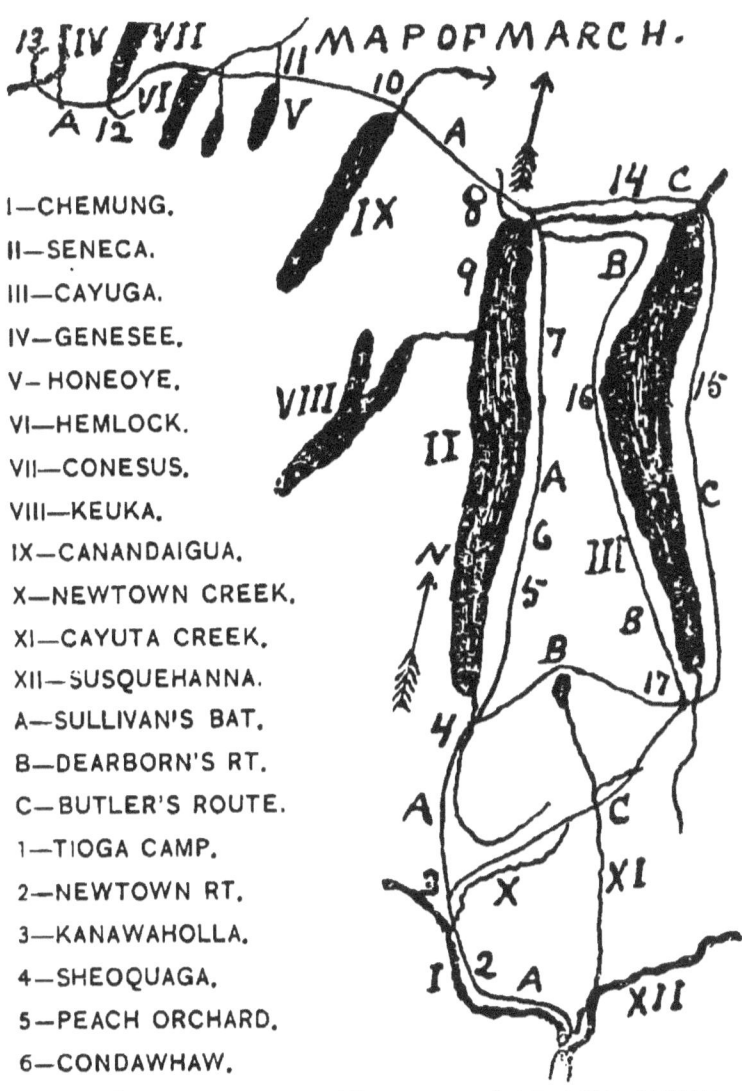

MAP OF MARCH.

I—CHEMUNG.
II—SENECA.
III—CAYUGA.
IV—GENESEE.
V—HONEOYE.
VI—HEMLOCK.
VII—CONESUS.
VIII—KEUKA.
IX—CANANDAIGUA.
X—NEWTOWN CREEK.
XI—CAYUTA CREEK.
XII—SUSQUEHANNA.
A—SULLIVAN'S BAT.
B—DEARBORN'S RT.
C—BUTLER'S ROUTE.
1—TIOGA CAMP.
2—NEWTOWN RT.
3—KANAWAHOLLA.
4—SHEOQUAGA.
5—PEACH ORCHARD.
6—CONDAWHAW.
7—KENDAIA. 8—KANADASEAGA. 9.—GOTHSEUNQUEAN.
10—KANANDAIGUA. 11—HANNEYAYE. 12—KANAGHSAWS.
13—CHENANDANAH. 14—SKOIYASE. 15—CHONODOTE.
16—SWAHYAWANA. 17—COREORGONEL.
ARROWS ON PRE-EMPTION LINE.

THE ANNAL.

The Annal of Olden Days is the outgrowth of several years of endeavor as a newspaper writer in the local field of the Lake Country, and the research for the facts presented was pursued with great care and diligent application. The work portrays the period of the pioneers of Central New York, and is designed to be a correct chronicle of the time. To one whose eighty years have been passed amid the scenes depicted, and another whose life has been about the lakes, these sketches are inscribed—Otis R. Corbett and Adelia B. Corbett, the parents of The Author.

THE LAKE COUNTRY.

AN ANNAL OF OLDEN DAYS IN CENTRAL NEW YORK.

The Lake Country is a region famed in song and story, of legendary lore that vests with poetic charm the placid lakes and tumbling streams, which render every part a pleasure ground. This picturesque land was the seat of empire of the Iroquois, from a time so remote that even tradition is silent as to the lighting of the first council-fire. Their trails along the shores have been obliterated; their hunting-grounds of hill and vale deforested; their remains rest in unknown graves by lake and stream. It embraces the waters of Central New York from the Onondaga to the Genesee. From the eastward to westward, in valleys extending north and south, its lakes range as follows: Otisco, Skaneateles, Owasco, Cayuga, Seneca, Keuka, Canandaigua, Honeoye, Canadice, Hemlock and Conesus.

THE LAKES.

The Lakes whose charms of wave and shore make beautiful the scenery of that section of New York State, southward of Ontario's waters, vary in length, breadth and depth, but occupy beds of similar trend and configuration, and doubtless great depressions of the earth, modified from original conformation by glacial action. Seneca and Cayuga hold superiority as to extent, and are also distinguished as occupying the central location of the Lake Country. Next in the order of size is Lake Keuka; then Canandaigua and Skaneateles, Owasco, Conesus, Hemlock, Honeoye, Canadice and Otisco.

Seneca Lake extends in a rock-riven valley, farther in the southward hills than adjoining lakes, and the fame of its glens and cascades is world-wide. From its surface, which is 447 feet above tide, the uplands rise from 500 to 1,000 feet, but arable to their summits. The lake is nearly forty miles in length, with an average breadth of less than two miles. The greatest width is 17,060 feet, off the outlet of Lake Keuka, and the deepest point of sounding, 612 feet, is three miles south of Lodi Landing. But three times in the memory of the present race of occupancy of its shores, have its waters been ice-fettered; they having at all other seasons billowed free beneath the wintry airs.

Cayuga Lake is separated from Seneca by a ridge, rising in its highest point to 1,257 feet above tide, and over the rock formations about its head, beautiful waterfalls mark the entrances to picturesque gorges. The length of the lake is about forty miles, and its elevation above tide is 387 feet. Its greatest width, 18,000 feet, is off Aurora, and its profoundest depth is 435 feet, at Kidder's Ferry, not in mid-stream, but near the west shore. The geological characteristics of the beds of Cayuga and Seneca are about the same; cliffs of shale and sandstone rising from head-waters to fertile slopes above, though the former has not an open valley to the southward, which is a feature of the latter.

Keuka Lake, which for a time suffered the loss of its aboriginal appellation in the commonplace designation of Crooked Lake, is nearly twenty miles in length, 718 feet above tide, and upwards of 200 feet deep. The two lakes, Canandaigua and Skaneateles, resemble each other in contour. Their lengths are about sixteen miles, but while the former is 668 feet above tide, the elevation of the latter is 860 feet. Owasco and Conesus Lakes are each some ten miles long; Hemlock and Honeoye Lakes are six miles in length, and Canadice and Otisco about four miles long. About all these waters, camp-fires glow in summertide, on shady points where wigwam-smoke arose in olden days.

THE IROQUOIS.

The Lake Country of Central New York perpetuates in the appellations of its romantic waters, the memories of a race whose council-fires have died forever from the shores. The Iroquois or Hodenosaunee, as they styled themselves, had domain from the Hudson to beyond the Genesee. The Mohawks held the eastern and the Senecas the western door of the "Long House," while to the Onondagas was entrusted the keeping of the central fire. Tradition names the Mohawks, the Onondagas and the Senecas as the elder nations, the Oneidas having diverged from the Onondagas and the Cayugas from the Senecas.

A chronicle of 1666, states that the Iroquois Nation formerly consisted of nine tribes, which occupied as many villages, finally collected together in order to sustain war more easily. The first tribe was that of the Tortoise, so-called from the belief that when the Master of Life made the earth he placed it on the tortoise. The second tribe was that of the Wolf, brother to the Tortoise, and on the question of war they deliberated together. The third tribe was that of the Bear; the fourth that of the Beaver, brother to the Bear; the fifth that of the Deer, the sixth that of the Potato, the seventh that of the Great Plover, the eighth that of the Little Plover, the ninth that of the Eagle. From this classification arose the totems of the tribes.

The League of the Iroquois was a confederation of Five Nations when first known to white men. The Onondagas were called "The Fathers of the Confederacy," from the belief that the idea of union originated with them. The Mohawks on consultation first assented, and became "The Eldest Brothers"; the Cayugas, "The Youngest Brothers"; the Oneidas, "The Heads of the Confederacy," and the Senecas, who were accorded two delegates to one each for the other tribes because of the greater number of warriors, were known as "The Watchmen." In 1722, the Tuscaroras, driven from the forest glades of the South, were admitted to the confederation, and thenceforth its annals were of the Six Nations.

The Senecas constituted by far the most powerful member of the Confederacy, and occupied not only the country along the Seneca Lake but westward to the Genesee and thence to the tributaries of the Ohio, while the other nations were mainly located about the waters that bear their names, the Tuscaroras having possessions near the Oneidas. An official report regarding the Indian tribes, made near the close of 1763, estimated the strength of the Senecas at 1,050 men, while all the remaining warriors of the confederation were enumerated at 900, apportioned among the several nations as follows: The Oneidas, 250; the Cayugas, 200; the Mohawks, 160; the Onondagas, 150; the Tuscaroras, 140.

THE EXPEDITION.

The Six Nations at the time of the Revolution were greatly advanced from the state of savagery, characteristic of the tribes of aborigines holding sway to the westward. Their territory had been left intact by the French and English during the wars ensuing in the struggle for supremacy on this continent, and throughout its extent were many flourishing villages in which log-cabins had taken the place of primitive wigwams, and where thrived upon the surrounding intervales, plantations of corn and beans and orchards of peach and apple trees.

The Great Council of the Iroquois had assured the Colonial authorities that neutrality would be observed in the contest then impending, but English influence becoming paramount in tribal affairs when the war began, rendered this pledge of no avail. The Confederation, however, mindful of preserving its national renown, prohibited the enemies of American Independence from establishing permanent fortifications within its borders, but extended aid to them by raising army food-supplies and inciting warrior bands to depredations on warpath or in ambuscade. The Indians thus allied with the British numbered some 1,200, of which a third at least were of the Seneca Nation.

The Colonies as late as March, 1778, endeavored to secure the good will of the Iroquois, but at the council called for the purpose the Cayugas were hardly represented and the Senecas not at all. Before the year was over, occurred the massacres of Wyoming and Cherry Valley, and the fact became impressed upon Congress that the savage foe must be subdued. In February, 1779, General Washington was authorized to take effective measures to that end, and in accordance with this determination a Military Expedition was planned against the Six Nations. The complete devastation of their land was contemplated, and the command of the avenging forces was entrusted to Major General John Sullivan.

The campaign was regarded by the Commander-in-Chief as of the greatest importance in the contest for freedom, and in his instructions concerning it he insisted upon two points to be observed, as follows: "The one is the necessity of pushing the Indians to the greatest practicable distance from their own settlements and our frontiers; to the throwing them wholly on the British enemy. The other is the making the destruction of their settlements so final and complete as to put it out of their power to derive the smallest succor from them in case they should attempt to return this season."

THE INVASION.

The Invasion of the country of the Six Nations by General Sullivan occurred in the autumn of 1779. The main army reached Tioga, as the point at the junction of the Chemung and the Susquehanna was called, on August 11th, and there established Fort Sullivan as a base of operations. The troops had marched from Easton on the Delaware to Wyoming on the Susquehanna, and thence up the river to the place of vantage, where they were joined on August 22nd, by the brigade in command of General James Clinton, which came down the Susquehanna from Otsego Lake.

The line of march into a wilderness swarming with savage warriors who alone knew its trails, was formed on August 26th. The Iroquois were met and routed at the Battle of Newtown on the 29th. The dreaded defiles of Catharine Creek were passed without molestation from the enemy, and September 1st found the army at Catharine's Town. Six days were required to reach and destroy the villages, the orchards and the cornfields along the eastern slope of Seneca Lake. From Kanadaseaga, which was entered the 7th, the route extended by the waters of Canandaigua, Honeoye, Hemlock and Conesus Lakes to the Genesee River. This was crossed on September 14th, and the army rested at the westward limit of its course.

The return march was begun on September 15th, and by the 19th the army had retraced the trail to Kanadaseaga. On the 20th, a detachment of 600 men under Colonel William Butler was sent to destroy the towns on the east side of Cayuga Lake, and Colonel Peter Gansevoort and 100 men were detached to Albany. The next day, a detachment of 200 men led by Colonel Henry Dearborn, left to devastate the west side of the Cayuga. The main army then returned over its out-going course, to the Chemung, arriving the 24th, where it awaited the detachments of Colonels Dearborn and Butler. The former joined on the 26th and the latter on the 28th, and September 30th the army again encamped at Tioga.

The country of the Cayugas like that of the Senecas was found to be deserted. Colonel Dearborn in his march up the west side of Cayuga Lake entered the village of Coreorgonel near its head, on September 24th. This was burned, and turning westward he trailed over the hills to Catharine's Town, arriving two days after General Sullivan's troops had passed through on their return southward. Colonel Butler in his course up the east side of the Cayuga, reached Coreorgonel on the 25th, the day after its destruction by Colonel Dearborn. He then proceeded southwesterly to the track of the main army, one man dying on the route.

THE ENGAGEMENT.

The Military force under command of General Sullivan has been variously estimated as to numbers, and was probably not far from 3,500 men. The First Brigade, led by General William Maxwell, was composed of New Jersey troops; the Second Brigade, General Enoch Poor, of New Hampshire and Massachusetts troops; the Third Brigade, General Edward Hand, of Pennsylvania troops, and the Fourth Brigade, General James Clinton, of New York troops. An artillery regiment was in command of Colonel Thomas Proctor, and an artillery detachment was led by Captain Isaiah Wool.

The Battle of Newtown was the only general engagement of the campaign. It was fought on Sunday, August 29th, on the left bank of the Chemung six miles below the site of Elmira, at a place well-chosen for defense or ambuscade, and now overlooked by a monument erected in 1879 in commemoration of the event. Intrenched behind breastworks artfully concealed in the pine and shrub-oak thicket, about 1,200 Indians, English and Tories awaited the approach of General Sullivan's battalions. The Iroquois, numbering some 1,000 warriors, were under the leadership of Joseph Brant or Thayendanegea, the War Chief of the Six Nations, and the whites were commanded by Colonel John Butler, notorious as the leader at Wyoming.

The Sabbath stillness which had prevailed for centuries over the hills about the valley of the Chemung, was then broken for the first time by the reverberations of cannon. It was the roar of artillery from the forces at their front and a detachment which had gained a position in their rear, that struck terror to the hearts of the Iroquois, and they precipitately fled, leaving eleven warriors and one female dead on the ground. Four of the whites were killed, and carried from the field. Two prisoners, a Tory and a Negro, fell into the hands of General Sullivan. In the official report of the action, he placed his loss at three killed and thirty-nine wounded. Five of the injured men died at Tioga soon after the battle.

The Expedition sustained loss of life at ambuscades previous and subsequent to the Battle of Newtown. The first occurred near the scene of that conflict, on August 13th, when troops that had left Tioga to burn the village of Chemung in order that it might not become a rendezvous of the enemy, were waylaid by the savage foe. Six men were killed and nine wounded, and later while destroying corn, one man was shot and five wounded by the Indians. The second ambuscade took place near the head of Conesus Lake, on September 13th. Of a scouting party, fifteen men were slain, eight escaped, and its leader, Lieutenant Thomas Boyd, and his sergeant, Michael Parker, were taken captive and put to death by torture.

THE DEVASTATION.

The Devastation of the land of the Senecas followed immediately upon the Battle of Newtown. The murk of that encounter yet rested over the valley, when the ominous cloud was augmented by the smoke of burning villages. The vanquished warriors nowhere made resistance, though up Seneca Lake came a force to support the routed horde, and one by one the Indian towns were desolated. There was much of the pageantry of war in the advance of General Sullivan's column of horse and foot. The guns numbered four three-pounders and a light brass piece called a cohorn, and morning and evening their roar warned the defeated Iroquois that flight alone was possible.

The mellowing haze of September brooded over the forest-covered slopes of Seneca and her sister lakes, as the flames of abandoned habitations marked the spots where destruction was rife in fields of corn, and orchards with their wealth of fruit were falling before the ranger's axe. On the plains of the Chemung, upon the intervales skirting the waters of the lakes, and in the valley of the Genesee flourished many a broad expanse of maize, but ripening only for the wanton hand of the despoiler. General Sullivan, in his report of the expedition, estimated that at a moderate computation 160,000 bushels of corn were destroyed with a vast quantity of vegetables of every kind, while the fruit trees felled to the ground numbered among the thousands.

The Indian towns doomed to destruction during the campaign were located on or near the sites of the present centers of population of the Lake Country. Before its waters were sighted and ere August had yet closed, the preliminary work of devastation had been accomplished along the Susquehanna and Chemung. Seven villages had been burned by General Clinton and three by the main army, before the meeting of forces at Tioga. Nine towns were destroyed about the Chemung; Newtown, Middletown, Kanawaholla of twenty houses on the site of Elmira, and Runonvea, near Big Flats, ending in flames on August 31st.

The despoliation of Catharine's Town with its wealth of corn and fruit, occurred soon after the arrival of the troops on September 1st; that of Peach Orchard, so-named for its fruits, the

3rd; Condawhaw, now North Hector, the 4th; Kendaia or Appletown, the 5th; Butler's Buildings and Kanadaseaga, near the foot of Seneca Lake, the 7th; Gothseunquean, west side of Seneca, and Skoi-yase, now Waterloo, the 8th; Kanandaigua, foot of Canandaigua Lake, the 10th; Hanneyaye, near Honeoye, the 11th; Kanaghsaws and Gathtsegwarohare, the 13th; Chenandanah or Genesee Castle, September 15th. Five towns were destroyed along the east side and as many on the west side of Cayuga Lake, before the burning of Coreorgonel on September 24th. This village of twenty-five houses was located three miles up Cayuga Inlet, and with it died the council-fires of the once powerful Catawba Nation.

THE ENCAMPMENTS.

The Encampments of the army after each day's destruction were usually on the sites of Indian villages, where the habitations furnished fire-wood, and the productions of fields of corn supplemented the short allowance of rations to which the troops had consented after the Battle of Newtown. The column tarried for a day after that contest, and also at each of the places of Catharine's Town, Kanadaseaga and Genesee Castle. These three towns were the most important of the Seneca Nation—the first from its location near the head of Seneca Lake; the second for its Council House, and the third as the western door of the figurative Long House of the Iroquois.

The village of Catharine's Town extended along the banks of Catharine Creek, a short distance to the southward of the site of Havana. Its Indian name was Sheoquaga, and among its thirty houses was included the dwelling of Queen Catharine Montour. Kanadaseaga was located upwards of a mile westward of the site of Geneva, in proximity to a stream, and consisted of some fifty houses. It was also called Seneca Castle, and was the place of residence of the Chief Sachem of the Seneca Nation. The great village of the Senecas, Genesee Castle or Chenandanah, was a town of about one hundred and thirty habitations, beautifully situated on the west shore of the Genesee River.

Three garrisons were established during the expedition, and at their locations encampments were made. The first garrison, at Fort Sullivan, consisted of 250 men in command of Colonel Israel Shreve. The artillery included two six-pounders and four more pieces after the Battle of Newtown, and was in charge of Captain Wool. At Hanneyaye, near the foot of Honeoye Lake, a block-house was garrisoned September 11th, and left in charge of Captain John Cumming till its evacuation on the 17th. Fort Reed was located where Newtown Creek joins Chemung River, on September 15th. It was a palisaded work in command of Captain John Reed, with 100 men and a three-pounder. There the army rested on its return, from September 24th to the 29th, and a feu-de-joie was an event of the 25th.

The longest encampment, from August 11th to the 26th, was at Tioga or

"The Gate," a place considered as of great importance by the Iroquois, and the location of an Indian village until its destruction by Colonel Hartley in 1778. From this strategical point extends the valleys of the Chemung and Susquehanna, and their diverging branches led into the heart of the country of the Six Nations. Fort Sullivan was constructed where the two rivers approach near each other, at about the center of the site of Athens, and included in the fortifications were four block-houses and a stockade. They were demolished on October 3rd, and the troops followed the Susquehanna southward.

THE BARBARITIES.

The Barbarities of warfare in the wilderness were committed alike by troops and Indians. The dead warriors of the Battle of Newtown were scalped when found, and the legs of two of the bodies were skinned, to be tanned and used as leggins by two officers during the campaign. The soldiers slain were buried on the field of action, and fires built above to conceal their resting places from prowling savages, but Indian graves were rifled by members of the army at Tioga, Kendaia and Genesee Castle, though contrary to orders. Lieutenant Boyd suffered the most cruel torture at his death, but his party had shot and scalped an Indian just before his capture.

An aged squaw was found at Catharine's Town, and treated by General Sullivan with much consideration, but she was not the sole habitant of its abandoned houses. A younger squaw was hidden in the corn, who pretended to be lame when discovered, but soon after disappeared. On the army's return, the old squaw was still in the cabin erected for her by the troops, with a quart of corn at her side, while the dead body of the younger squaw lay a short distance away, pierced by a bullet evidently from a ranger's rifle. The old squaw preferred remaining with a supply of provisions, to going with the army, and it is hoped that she was rescued by her race before the snows fell o'er the scene of desolation.

At a deserted village on the west side of Cayuga Lake, Colonel Dearborn on his trail of desolation, found three squaws and a young Indian who was a cripple. Two of the squaws were made prisoners, leaving the other, an old crone, and the lad inmates of the only habitation of the town that was spared from the flames. The troops marched on, but it was reported among the members of the main army after the detachment had joined its forces at Fort Reed, that soldiers, disobeying the commands, had returned, and fastening the door of the cabin upon those within, fiendishly applied the torch and burned it to the ground.

The captives of the campaign were few, more having been released from the Indians than taken by the troops. At Kendaia, Luke Swetland awaited the arrival of the army. He had been captured at Wyoming, and made a member of an Indian family. A boy about three years old, evidently stolen from some frontier home, was found at Kanadaseaga, naked and greatly emaciated, the only sharer of his solitude, a chicken with which he was playing. He was adopted by an officer, but died two years afterwards. While at Genesee Castle, a white woman with a child came to the army. Her husband had been slain and she made prisoner in an Indian raid. The child died on the return march. She became the wife of Roswell Franklin, the first settler of Cayuga county.

THE RETREAT.

The Iroquois in their retreat from homes and hunting-grounds were frequently but a few hours' march in advance of the military forces. The old squaw of Catharine's Town stated to General Sullivan, that after a spirited debate as to flight or battle, Butler and the Tories left in the boats, while early the next day the women and children were sent away, the warriors then returning and remaining until nearly sunset, departing but a short time before the troops entered the town. The released captive of Kendaia, said the defeat at Newtown had been announced by Indian runners proclaiming the death halloo, in less than twenty-four hours after the conflict.

Many evidences of the impression wrought upon the Indians by this disaster to their race were visible along the route, but the most striking were the finding of dogs hung up on poles some twelve feet high, as sacrifices to the God of War, and the discovery of an inscription on a tree near Catharine's Town, which was chronicled by an adept in wood-lore as follows: "This day found a tree marked 1779, Thandagana, the English of which is Brant, twelve men marked on it with arrows pierced through them signifying the number they had lost in the action of the 29th ultimo—a small tree was twisted round like a rope and bent down, which signified that if we drove and distressed them yet we would not conquer them."

The spirit of the Senecas, the Watchmen of the Confederacy of the Six Nations, had been broken, and far from their forest haunts they congregated only to have their numbers decimated by disease. In inadequate quarters about Niagara, the pestilence finished the desolation of the Nation, begun by the forces of General Sullivan, whose home-returning was marked by the buoyancy of heart arising from victory. Wearied by toilsome marches, yet inspirited by success, the troops arrived at Tioga on September 30th, having suffered a loss of but forty-one men during the campaign, which really closed with the burning of an Indian town located near Painted Post, by a detachment sent up the Chemung from Fort Reed, on the 27th.

The army found no opportunity for celebration, until encamped at Fort Reed, where on September 25th, occurred a memorable demonstration in honor of the Thirteen States and the achievements of the expedition. A salute of thirteen guns was followed by a running fire through the lines of infantry, and cheering from the whole body of troops. Five oxen were barbecued on the occasion, and in one brigade thirteen fires were kept burning and thirteen toasts were drank. The fort was razed on the 29th, and the following day the army entered Fort Sullivan with military parade, to the strains of martial music and the roar of artillery. The display preceded a jollification, which did not entirely cease until the day of evacuation, Sunday, October 3rd.

THE CHRONICLE.

The Chronicle of events of the Military Expedition was made by many of those who participated in its dangers. In addition to the official report of the campaign by General Sullivan, several journals were kept, some in part, others in entirety, and most of them in detail. Each observer evidenced his inclinations in his notations, and thus the scenery, the physical features and the productions of grain and fruit were themes of full descriptions. By research of these and other records were collated the facts presented in the foregoing articles, which briefly outline the occurrences of this epoch in Lake Country lore.

The scenery was an object of especial note, the successive views unfolding before the advancing column in all their pristine beauty. The pellucid waters of Lakes Seneca and Cayuga, mirroring wooded slopes broken only by the silvery sheen of waterfalls, evoked expressions of deep admiration. The thrifty orchards, the abundance of maize, the fine forest growth indicating excellence of soil, the natural meadows on which fed horses and cattle were subjects of comment. One mentioned the killing of many large rattlesnakes; another the capture of a salmon upwards of two feet in length, while a third in remarking upon the great quantities of wild grapes growing near Canandaigua Lake, foreshadowed the vineyard acreage of today.

The Indian houses varied in degrees of finish from the frail construction of bark to the substantial structure of logs, and were built about the village site with no observance of order. The dwellings, according to one account, might have been very comfortable had any convenience existed for the smoke to escape except a hole through the roof. One of the twenty habitations, however, of Kendaia was provided with a chimney. Queen Catharine's palace was a gambrel-roofed house about thirty feet long and eighteen wide. A Dutch family lived in Catharine's Town, and departed with the Indians, leaving behind a number of feather beds. The best constructed Seneca village destroyed was Kanandaigua, consisting of twenty-three large houses, mostly new.

An Indian grave was usually a shallow resting place in which the dead encased in bark, moldered away in an unmarked mound, but o'er the remains of a chief a painted monumental post was ofttimes reared. Over some of the old graves about Tioga were raised mounds of earth to the height of four or six feet, the bodies having first been laid but slightly beneath the surface of the ground. Tombs of different construction from those elsewhere were found at Kendaia, the most notable evidently that of a chief. Covering the body was a casement about four feet high, with the sides and ends curiously painted in many colors, and over all was a shed of bark to protect the memorial from the elements.

THE TRADITIONS.

The Traditions attendant upon this martial advance into the Lake Country, will ever remain themes of interest to all dwellers within its borders. Along the trail of the invader, legend has located occurrences not recorded by the chroniclers of the event, but which in general are doubtless true. Many who accompanied General Sullivan on the march which blazed the way for the advance of civilization, returned at the close of the Revolution to rear their homes in this pleasant land, and to their recount of recollections is evidently due many of the incidents that have remained unwritten annals of that olden time.

A beetling cliff, along the rocky shore extending for some miles down the eastern side of Seneca Lake from its head, is known as Painted Rocks. It was said by old settlers to have borne Indian paintings on its face in commemoration of a Seneca Chief, who there met death in a skirmish with the van-guard of General Sullivan's troops. No record of such an encounter is extant, but a scouting party is known to have been sent to the lake from Catharine's Town, while the main army rested on September 2nd, and shots may have been exchanged with warriors in ambush in the thickets of that locality, with results unknown to the rangers, yet fatal to the skulking foe.

The appellation of Poney Hollow, through which flows a tributary to Cayuta Creek, arose from some fact connected with the return march of the detachment in command of Colonel Butler. The course from the head of Cayuga Lake was up the Inlet, down the stream of Poney Hollow, and thence across country to the head-waters of Newtown Creek, which was followed to the Chemung. The derivation of the name of Horseheads is apparent, yet the record that horses of the expedition were killed at that point is quite obscure. The frequent breaking down of the gun-carriages probably gave rise to the tradition of a lost cannon, for all the field-pieces taken out on the trail were returned by the troops to Tioga.

The western slope of Seneca in greater part and the picturesque shores of Lake Keuka in entirety, had their primeval solitudes unbroken by the army of invasion, and Indian burial places now mark the spots where villages existed then or at an earlier date. One located at the head of the West Branch of Keuka, rivals Canoga in the claim of having been the birthplace of Red Jacket, while the smoke of others arose from the head and foot of the lake. An Iroquois village once occupied the site of Watkins, for Indian graves are many to the eastward of the entrance to Watkins Glen, and apple-trees planted by aborigines and spared by the troops because not found, flourished above them and furnished fruit for the pioneers.

THE COMMANDERS.

The Commanders of the Expedition against the Indians were not only experienced in war, but men of marked ability as well as valor, most of them having become distinguished in civil life before the performance of meritorious service in the Revolution. The roster of officers included many names high on the roll of national honor, only those having been selected to lead the perilous undertaking who were known to have especial fitness for the work, and when the campaign was completed lustre had invariably been added to their fame.

The Commander-in-Chief, Major General John Sullivan, was born of Irish parentage in Somersworth, N. H., February 18th, 1740. He was a member of the Provincial Assembly in 1774, and a delegate to the Continental Congress the year following. He was appointed Brigadier General in June, 1775, and Major General in July, 1776. He participated in the battles of Long Island, the Brandywine, Germantown and others, but his greatest achievement was the successful leadership of the campaign in the Indian country. After the Revolution, General Sullivan represented New Hampshire in Congress, and was Chief Magistrate of the State for several terms. He was appointed by President Washington, Judge of the United States District Court of New Hampshire, in 1789, and held the office until his death, January 23rd, 1795.

Brigadier-General James Clinton was born August 9th, 1736, in Orange county, N. Y., where his death occurred December 22nd, 1812. He was the son of Colonel Charles Clinton, the brother of Governor George Clinton and the father of Governor DeWitt Clinton. After attaining an admirable Revolutionary record he held important civil positions. Brigadier-General Edward Hand was born in Ireland, December 31st, 1744, and died in Lancaster county, Pa., September 4th, 1802. He acquired a knowledge of the Indian country while in command at Pittsburg, previous to the Expedition. Brigadier-General William Maxwell was also of Irish descent, but little is known of his personal history. He died in November, 1798. Brigadier-General Enoch Poor resided most of his life at Exeter, N. H. He was born in Andover, Mass., June 21st, 1736, and died September 9th, 1780.

Colonel Henry Dearborn was born in Hampton, N. H., in March, 1751, and died in Roxbury, Mass., June 6th, 1829. He was Secretary of War under President Jefferson. Colonel William Butler was of Irish descent, his family having settled in Cumberland county, Pa., prior to 1760. He died at Pittsburg in 1789. Colonel Peter Gansevoort was of a Knickerbocker family, and born in Albany July 17th, 1749. His death occurred after receiving many honors, July 2nd, 1812. Colonel Thomas Proctor was born in Ireland, but in early life came to Philadelphia, where he died March 16th, 1806. The ill-fated Lieutenant Thomas Boyd was from Derry, Pa., and but twenty-two years old at his untimely death.

THE SACHEMS.

The Sachems of the Six Nations were men of prowess and sagacity, as well when driven from the Lake Country as in the past. Giengwahtoh, or "He who goes in the smoke," the most powerful Sachem of his time, had his home in Kanadaseaga from which he fled to Niagara. He had the honor, accorded to no other, of carrying the brand by which the council fires were lighted. As Civil Chief of the Senecas his word was law, and his decisions when convened in council were never questioned. His descendant, Young King, allied his warriors with the forces of the United States during the War of 1812.

The War Chief of the Confederacy was Joseph Brant, a descendant of a Sachem of the Mohawks and called by the Indians, Thayendanegea. Among the Iroquois, in peace the voice of the principal Sachem was potential, in war he was but a counselor while the War Chief became the dictator. Brant embraced his opportunity and led the warriors to the fray with savage ferocity, but only to final defeat. He was the implacable foe of the Colonies, and his name became the synonym of slaughter to the settlers of the border. Yet withal, he was a man of ability and high accomplishments for his race. He died on British soil, November 24th, 1807, at the age of sixty-five years.

The eloquence characteristic of the Iroquois had its greatest exponent among the Senecas in Sagoyewatha, or Red Jacket. He was yet a young man when his Nation was driven from lakeside haunts, and it was not until the great councils following the war, that his oratorical powers gave him distinction. He lived to see his people despoiled of their lordly domain, and their clans scattered to pent up reservations. As a means of preservation of his race, he urged adherence to old customs and the upholding of the ancient belief. Red Jacket died in the Seneca village near Buffalo, January 20th, 1830, at the estimated age of seventy years. The site of his supposed birthplace, was marked at Canoga on Cayuga Lake, in 1891.

The Seneca Chief Cornplanter or Gaantuaha, like Red Jacket was a natural orator, but of greater age at the period of invasion, and was also a warrior of prominence. Both spake burning words in behalf of their Nation at the treaty of peace with the United States in 1784, and ever after each remained the firm friend of the government. Their rivalry for leadership among their people continued long, the latter finally triumphing. Cornplanter died March 7th, 1836, aged upwards of one hundred years. The closing scenes of his life were among the Allegany clans of the Senecas, whom he endeavored to bring into a state of civilization.

THE WOMEN.

The Women of the Iroquois were influential factors in tribal affairs, and in the household regulated matters altogether, prescribing the locations of cabins and dictating removals. It was an equitable feature of Indian polity that the lands belonged to those who tilled them as well as the warriors who defended them, and hence in treaties as to their disposal the opinions of the women were treated with deference. At the great council of the Six Nations and the United States, in Canandaigua, the autumn of 1794, women were allowed to express their sentiments before the assemblage.

The regal titles of two women are prominent in the annals of the Military Expedition, though about them clusters more or less of tradition. Queen Esther is a name that will ever be inseparably connected with the atrocities of Wyoming. She is said to have been the granddaughter of Madame Montour, the daughter of French Margaret, and a sister of Queen Catharine. Her only son was slain at Wyoming, and her unparalleled barbarities at the massacre, the tomahawking of prisoners, were to avenge his death. Her village, located on the Susquehanna near the junction of the Chemung, was burned by Colonel Thomas Hartley shortly after this event, and her deeds were no more of disaster throughout the valley-side.

Catharine Montour has her name perpetuated in stream and valley about the site of Sheoquaga, the Iroquois village over which she ruled as Queen Catharine. The statements as to her life are as of romance. Her reputed father was one of the early French governors of Canada, and her maternal lineage traced from Madame Montour, a noted personage in the Colonial history of Pennsylvania. She was taken captive in a war-raid of the Six Nations and adopted by the Senecas, a Chief of that Nation, Thomas Hudson or Telenemut, becoming her husband. Of her children little is known, save that she had two daughters and one son, Amochol. After the flight of her people, she passed her life amid the scenes about Niagara.

The "White Woman of the Genesee" was a noted personage among the Senecas during the Revolution. Her name was Mary Jemison before her marriage, first to a Delaware Chief and after his death to a Seneca Chief. When a child, in 1754, her parents, two brothers and other members of the family had been murdered by the Indians, and she taken captive. As time progressed she became thoroughly an Iroquois in all her habits, and she did not discard her Indian costume even after civilization had changed the valley. She died about the year 1825, rich in flocks and herds as well as in lands.

THE TREATIES.

The Six Nations driven from the country about the lakes by the Military Expedition of 1779, returned not again to hold supremacy along their waters, and though divested of the prestige of power by the campaign, the hatchet was not formally buried by the warring element of the Confederacy until the council with representatives of the United States, at Fort Stanwix, on the site of Rome, in the fall of 1784. By that treaty of peace the Indians were received under the protection of the government, and secured in the possession of the lands of which they were then occupants.

Council fires burned at deliberations

between the Iroquois and the United States, in November, 1790, at Tioga, and again in June, 1791, at Painted Post. These assemblages were convoked by the government for the purpose of diverting the attention of the Indians of New York from the wars of the western tribes, and the endeavors to that end were successful. The last general council held by the United States and the Confederacy occurred during the autumn of 1794, at Canandaigua, with the result of the establishment of relations upon a permanent basis. Reservations to the Oneidas, Onondagas and Cayugas were confirmed, and the boundaries fully determined to the country of the still numerous Seneca Nation.

The Treaty of Big Tree, on the site of Geneseo, in September, 1797, extinguished the title of the Six Nations to their ancient possessions, with the exception of reservations that at councils in subsequent years were released or greatly lessened in area. Though not principals in the transaction, both the United States and Massachusetts were represented at the negotiations, which were conducted with the Seneca Nation by capitalists, the precursors of settlement. The great purchase of land consummated, included about two-thirds of that portion of the State west of the Pre-emption Line, the rest having been obtained at a treaty with the Indians, in July, 1788, at Kanadaseaga.

The Senecas now occupy two reservations—the Allegany of 30,469 acres, and the Cattaraugus of 21,680 acres. Their population was 2,139 in 1889. The Tuscaroras have 6,249 acres near Niagara River, and numbered that year 409. The Tonawandas, a branch of the Senecas, have 7,547 acres, occupied by about 500 Indians. The Onondagas, yet recognized as leaders of the Six Nations, have 7,300 acres, on which reside some 450 Indians; about 125 of the nation being with the Senecas. The Oneidas are in Wisconsin, except 178 near Oneida Lake; 75 with the Onondagas, and 30 with the Tuscaroras. The Cayugas removed to Indian Territory, save 160 with the Senecas and a few with the Tonawandas. The Mohawks left the State for Canada during the Revolution.

THE PRE-EMPTION.

The Revolution closed with a dispute as to extent of territory, pending between the States of New York and Massachusetts. The colonial charter of the latter conveyed the region between its north and south boundaries from the Atlantic to the Pacific, and the subsequent charter of New York conflicted with this grant. An amicable arrangement of the matter was effected in December, 1786, Massachusetts then relinquishing the claim to jurisdiction but retaining the right of the pre-emption of the soil from the Indians, to that portion of New York west of a designated survey, thenceforth known as the Pre-emption Line.

The right of purchase from the Six Nations thus acquired by Massachusetts extended over a tract of some 7,000,000 acres, and in 1787, the whole claim was sold by that State to Oliver Phelps and Nathaniel Gorham for $1,000,000. At

Kanadaseaga the following year, they secured title to the eastern third of the land, an area extending in a body from Pennsylvania to Lake Ontario, and from the Pre-emption to a line parallel with and twelve miles west of the Genesee River. The remainder of the tract reverted to Massachusetts, and was re-sold to Robert Morris, of Philadelphia. After the procurement of the Indian title, at the council in 1797, at Big Tree, it became mainly the property of the Holland Land Company.

The Pre-emption Line extends from the eighty-second milestone on the boundary between New York and Pennsylvania, northward to Lake Ontario, and is the most prominent landmark connected with the settlement of the Lake Country. It is on the meridian of Washington, strikes Seneca Lake at Dresden, passes east of Geneva and to the head of Great Sodus Bay, dividing the counties of Chemung and Steuben and Seneca and Ontario. The survey of the true line, known as the "New Pre-emption Line," was made in 1795, under direction of

Major Hoops assisted by Andrew Ellicott and Augustus Porter. A vista thirty feet wide was opened through the forest by a corps of axe-men, and signals were employed in the course over Seneca.

The "Old Pre-emption Line" was run at an earlier date, and through the influence of land-owners who desired it located to the west of Geneva, the surveyors did not follow the true meridian. The deviation began soon after leaving the Pennsylvania border, and gradually continued until the outlet of Lake Keuka was crossed. Then the line bore more to the westward till opposite the foot of Seneca Lake, when a northerly course was resumed and Lake Ontario reached about three miles west of Great Sodus Bay. The strip of territory between the two surveys was called "The Gore," and the State having made grants of the tract, compensation lands were allotted as an equivalent, on the establishment of the true line.

THE TITLES.

The Titles to the lands of Central-Western New York are derived from the Massachusetts Pre-emption, the Military Tract, and Patents to land companies and individuals. The subdivisions of the Massachusetts lands were the Phelps and Gorham purchase, not reverting, of 2,600,000 acres; Holland Company's purchase, 3,600,000; the Morris Reserve, 500,000; Sterritt tract, 150,000; Connecticut tract, 100,000; Church tract, 100,000; Triangular tract, 87,000; Morris creditors' tract, 58,570; Cragie, Ogden and Cottinger tracts, each of 50,000; Forty-thousand acre tract. Massachusetts also had title to the "Boston Ten Towns" of 230,400 acres, now in Broome and Tioga counties.

The Military Tract consisted of twenty-eight townships, each containing some 60,000 acres, divided into 100 lots. The Onondagas in 1788, ceded to the State all their country except a reservation, and the tract thus acquired and one adjoining it on the west were set apart for bounty lands to Revolutionary soldiers, who were required to make settlement within seven years from January 1st, 1790. The area of the Military Tract included all the territory within the original limits of Onondaga county, and now constituting the counties of Onondaga, Cortland, Cayuga and Seneca and parts of Oswego, Wayne, Tompkins and Schuyler. The southwestern township was Hector, which of the entire twenty-eight, alone retains its first boundaries.

The Patent granted to John W. Watkins and Royal Flint, with whom were associated other residents of New York City, in the year 1794, included upwards of 300,000 acres located to the southward of Seneca and Cayuga Lakes. The application had been made as early as 1791, for the purchase of all the unlocated part of the tract, which was bounded on the west by the Pre-emption Line, on the south by the Township of Chemung, on the east by the "Boston Ten Towns," on the north by the Military Tract to the head of Seneca Lake, and thence to the Pre-emption, by a tract sold to James Watson. Of the several locations of lands then existing within the limits of the purchase, the largest was that of Ezra L'Hommedieu of 5,440 acres, about the site of Havana.

The James Watson tract extended along Seneca Lake, northward from its head, its boundary upon the west the Pre-emption Line, and was of an area estimated at over 50,000 acres. He and others also bought 14,550 acres of the unappropriated lands in the Township of Chemung. Along Seneca Lake, about the outlet to Lake Keuka, James Parker in behalf of the followers of Jemima Wilkinson, known as the Friends, purchased some 12,000 acres. North of this tract, Seth Reed and Peter Ryckman had secured title of the State to 16,000 acres, located southward from the foot of Seneca Lake between its western shore and the Pre-emption Line. The patent was issued before the first survey, and fully accounts for the deviation of course of the line then run.

THE ESTATES.

The Land Companies disposed of their possessions, either by allotment among members or by sale to investors in large estates, who transferred to purchasers of small holdings. The cost to settlers was slight even after several changes of title, because of the original low prices of land. The Watson purchase was at the rate of three shillings and sevenpence per acre; the Watkins and Flint patent, at three shillings and fourpence, the State reserving all gold and silver mines and five acres in every 100 for highways; the Parker purchase, at two shillings and one shilling and sixpence. The lands of the Military Tract in township lots, were rated at one shilling and eightpence per acre.

The Watkins and Flint purchase was surveyed so as to create twelve townships, each including four sections. The Watson tract was divided into great lots, containing from twelve to sixteen small lots of 100 acres in extent. Among those acquiring estates through the granting of these patents, and by subsequent purchase or inheritance, were Jonathan Lawrence, Robert C. Livingston, John Lamb, John Ireland, Robert C. Johnson, Joshua Brooks, Charles Wilkes, John S. Livingston, Lewis Simonds, Harmon Pumpelly, Elisha Bondinot, John L. Clarkson, James Pumpelly, Samuel W. Johnson and Isaac Q. Leake. Dr. Samuel Watkins succeeded his brothers, John W. and Charles Watkins, as landed proprietor at the head of Seneca Lake.

The lands of the Phelps and Gorham purchase were placed on sale to settlers as early as 1789, when the first regular land-office in America was opened at Canandaigua by Oliver Phelps. The system of survey by townships and ranges then inaugurated, became the basis for laying out all new lands of the United States. Each township sold by selection was accompanied by another chosen by lot, and the same amounts in payment were required for both. A large portion of this tract passed into the hands of William Pulteney and others of London, whose agent, Charles Williamson, in 1792 and following years, unsuccessfully endeavored to establish the metropolis of the Genesee Country on the site of Bath.

The Township of Chemung was created by the Legislature in March, 1788, and hence was the first civil division about the Pre-emption Line, which was its west boundary. The south limit was the line between New York and Pennsylvania; the north having been some ten miles distant and parallel therewith, and its east boundary following the courses of Owego Creek and Susquehanna River. Previous to its erection, various land-owners had become possessed of estates within its borders, ranging in extent from 1,000 acres up to the many thousands of individuals and associations, but after the survey then authorized, the allotments were not less than 100 nor more than 1,000 acres, purchased at the price of one shilling and sixpence per acre.

THE COUNTIES.

The Counties of Ontario, Tioga, Steuben, Cayuga, Seneca, Tompkins, Livingston, Yates, Wayne, Chemung and Schuyler extend their areas at present over the section of the State affected by the invasion of the land of the Iroquois, in 1779. Their dates of formation, in the order as given, cover a period commencing ten years after that event and continuing until three-quarters of a century had elapsed. Albany county, created November 1st, 1683, by subsequent statutes was made to comprise all the colony of New York, north and west of its other limits. Montgomery county, as "Tryon county," March 12th, 1772, was set off to the westward of the Delaware River.

Ontario county was formed from Montgomery, January 27th, 1789, and then included all of New York west of the Pre-emption Line. Its great dismemberment occurred March 20th, 1802, when the country beyond the Genesee River was organized as Genesee county, although Steuben county had previously been taken off. It was not until 1823, and after further territory had been furnished for portions of Livingston, Monroe, Wayne and Yates counties, that boundaries became fixed. Steuben county was created from Ontario, March 18th, 1796, and after contributing to parts of Allegany, Livingston, Yates and Schuyler, its area, which is still the greatest of the counties of Western New York, became of permanent character in 1854.

Tioga county was set off from Montgomery, February 16th, 1791. It extended as far east as the Delaware River and westward to the Pre-emption Line, between the State of Pennsylvania and the county of Herkimer, also formed from Montgomery the same day. Parts of Chenango and Tompkins and the entire counties of Broome and Chemung were taken from the territory of Tioga, previous to the close of 1836. Onondaga county, which included the Military Tract, was organized from Herkimer, March 5th, 1794. On March 8th, 1799, its western portion became Cayuga county, from which was taken Seneca in 1804, and a part of Tompkins in 1817, leaving its bounds thenceforth intact.

Thus, Ontario, Tioga, Steuben and Cayuga were the counties of the lakes in 1800.

Seneca county was created from Cayuga, March 29th, 1804, and originally comprised that portion of the Military Tract west of Cayuga Lake. Its southern towns went to Tompkins in 1817, and its northern part to Wayne in 1823. Tompkins county was formed from Cayuga and Seneca, April 17th, 1817. Towns were annexed from Tioga, March 22nd, 1822, and territory set off to Schuyler in 1854. Livingston county was organized from Ontario and Genesee, February 23rd, 1821, and in 1846 and '56, portions of Allegany were added; Yates county, from Ontario, February 5th, 1823, and towns were annexed from Steuben, April 6th, 1824; Wayne county, from Ontario and Seneca, April 11th, 1823; Chemung county, from Tioga, March 29th, 1836; Schuyler county, from Chemung, Steuben and Tompkins, April 17th, 1854.

THE OFFICIALS.

The Officials of Ontario county were the first in Western New York, and as follows: Judge, Oliver Phelps; Clerk, Nathaniel Gorham; Sheriff, Judah Coit; Surrogate, John Cooper. A circuit court was held at Patterson's Inn, Geneva, in June, 1793, and a court of common pleas at the house of Nathaniel Sanbern in Canandaigua, in November, 1794. The first Justices of the Peace west of the Pre-emption Line were Asa Ransom and William Rumsey appointed in December, 1801. Steuben's sole county-seat was at Bath until 1853, when the creation of two jury districts caused the erection of county buildings at Corning. The first officials were: Judge, William Kersey; Clerk, George D. Cooper; Sheriff, William Dunn; Surrogate, Stephen Ross.

Tioga was formed a half-shire county by the act of organization, which provided that the courts should be held alternately at Chenango, now Binghamton, and at Newtown Point, now Elmira. The half-shire was abolished upon the creation of Broome county in 1806, and soon afterwards Spencer village became the county-seat of Tioga, which in 1812 was again divided into two jury districts, with courts at Elmira and Spencer. The court-house at the latter place was burned in 1821, and the following year Owego was designated in its stead, to become the sole county-seat on setting off Chemung county. The first officials of Tioga were: Judge, Abram Miller; Clerk, Thomas Nicholson; Sheriff, James McMasters; Surrogate, John Mersereau.

Cayuga county courts up to 1808, when new county buildings were occupied at Auburn, were held at Aurora, on the east shore of Cayuga Lake. In 1803, Daniel D. Tompkins there presided at a circuit court and court of oyer and terminer, at which an Indian was tried and convicted of the murder of Ezekial Crane, Jr. The first officials of Cayuga were: Judge, Seth Phelps; Clerk, Benjamin Ledyard; Sheriff, Joseph Annin; Surrogate, Glen Cuyler; District Attorney, William Stuart. The county-seat of

Seneca was at Ovid from 1804 to 1817, and then at Waterloo until 1822, when two jury districts were created and courts held alternately at each place. The first officials were: Judge, Cornelius Humphrey; Clerk, Silas Halsey; Sheriff, William Smith; Surrogate, Jared Sandford.

Tompkins county's first officials were: Judge, Oliver C. Comstock; Clerk, Archer Green; Sheriff, Henry Bloom; Surrogate, Andrew Bruyn. Livingston county—Judge, Moses Hayden; Clerk, James Ganson; Sheriff, Gideon T. Jenkins; Surrogate, James Roseburgh. Yates county—Judge, William M. Oliver; Clerk, Abraham H. Bennett; Sheriff, James P. Robinson; Surrogate, Abraham P. Vosburgh; District Attorney, James Taylor. Wayne county—Judge and Surrogate, John S. Talmadge; Clerk, Isaiah J. Richardson; Sheriff, Hugh Jameson; District Attorney, William H. Adams. Chemung county—Judge, Joseph L. Darling; Clerk, Isaac Baldwin; Sheriff, Albert A. Beckwith; Surrogate, Lyman Covill; District Attorney, Andrew K. Gregg. Schuyler county—

Judge and Surrogate, Simeon L. Rood; Clerk, A. S. Newcomb; Sheriff, John J. Swartwood; District Attorney, Lewis F. Riggs.

THE PIONEERS.

The Pioneers included representatives of every State in the Union and nearly every country in Europe, all endeavoring to advance the interests of community, and from this commingling of character has developed the people, whose efforts to-day are worthily conserving the wealth of resource of their pleasant heritage about the lakes. The deeds of this advance guard are dimmed already by the mists of years; their works have followed them to the obscurity of time; like the race which they succeeded, their remains are moldering in neglected resting places. They planned, they labored, they accomplished, laying well the foundations of prosperity.

Indian traders led the van of settlement in the Southern Tier, Amos Draper thus establishing himself on the site of Owego in 1785, and William Harris at Painted Post in 1787. The former was joined by James, William and Robert McMaster, John McQuigg, William Taylor, John Nealey and William Wood, and the latter by David Fuller, Eli Mead and Van Nye, Samuel, Frank and Arthur Erwin, Howell Bull and John Evans. The first settlers on the Chemung were William Wynkoop, William and Elijah Buck, Daniel McDowell, Joseph Bennett, Thomas Burt, Enoch Warren and son. Colonel John Hendy located on the site of Elmira; Frederick Calkins and Benjamin Eaton at Corning, followed by Benjamin and Peleg Gorton, Ephraim Patterson and others.

Among the pioneers on the town sites, up to the close of 1790, were the following: Geneva, Seth Reed, Peter Ryckman, Horatio Jones, Asa Ransom, Lark Jennings, Doctor Benton, Peter Bortle and Jonathan Whitney; Canandaigua, Nathaniel Gorham, Jr., Frederick Saxton, Joseph Smith, Israel Chapin and Benjamin Gardner; Lyons, Nicholas and William Stansell and John Featherly; Naples, Samuel Parish and William

Watkins and brothers; Geneseo, James and William Wadsworth; Honeoye, Peter Pitts; Palmyra, John Swift; Waterloo, John Greene; Ovid, Andrew Dunlap; Ithaca, Jacob Yaple, Isaac Dumond and Peter Hinepaw; Watkins, David Culver, Daniel Smyth and John Dow; Havana, Silas Wolcott, William McClure, Phineas Bowers and George Mills.

The first settler of the Military Tract was Job Smith, on the site of Seneca Falls in 1787. He was joined by Lawrence Van Clief. The pioneer of Cayuga county, Roswell Franklin, died at Aurora in 1791. Mrs. Jedediah Holmes died near the site of Dresden in 1788; Caleb Walker in Canandaigua, and Rachel Allen at the head of Cayuga Lake, in 1790; George Dunlap, near Ovid in 1791; Mrs. Job Smith, at Seneca Falls in 1792; Elizabeth Barber and Jean M'Gahen, at the head of Seneca Lake in 1793; Ichabod Patterson, on the site of Corning in 1794. These graves of the wilderness, with the exception of the battle-slain, were doubtless the first made in the land, where previously had rested but the dead of the Iroquois.

THE SETTLEMENT.

The Settlement of the Lake Country was fully underway within ten years after the campaign against the Six Nations, and among the home-seekers were many who had been numbered in the army of invasion. In their work of devastation, the troops had noted the attractions of the region and the advantages that awaited but the hand of enterprise. Indications were unmistakable that by direction of white men, had been planted the fields of corn and reared the cabins of hewn logs which were features of the villages, but it was no less apparent, that at a far earlier time the seeds of the trees of fruit had been placed in the receptive soil by the Iroquois.

The treaty of 1784 prepared the way for occupancy by settlers, but it was not until a year or so later that clearings were commenced within the wilderness. Two lines of pioneers trailed from the bounds of civilization into the broad expanse of primeval forest, from which the Indian had been driven but where still lurked beasts of prey. Those from Eastern New York and the rocky hillsides of New England arrived by way of the Mohawk River, while the thoroughfare from the plains of New Jersey and Southern Pennsylvania was the pathway followed by the soldiers of Sullivan. The meeting place of these advancing hosts is perpetuated in the name of Penn Yan, midway of the northern and southern limits of the land of the lakes.

The settlers from Pennsylvania established themselves along the Susquehanna and Chemung, within the borders of New York, as early as 1786, an Indian trader occupying the site of Owego the preceding year. In 1787, a trader settled at Painted Post, while the same year people from New England located on the site of Geneva, and log-houses were erected at Seneca Falls and about the outlet of Lake Keuka. In 1788, settlements were made on the sites of Elmira, Corning, Havana, Watkins and Canandaigua; in 1789, Horseheads, Ithaca,

Ovid, Aurora, Waterloo, Penn Yan, Honeoye, Lyons and Palmyra; in 1790, Naples and Geneseo; in 1791, Newark and Wayne; in 1792, Bath and Trumansburg; in 1793, Auburn and Hammondsport.

Several of the locations on present centers of population, for a year or two were marked by lone cabins, but the tide of incoming travel continually augmented in volume, and in 1793, the inhabitants of the Genesee Lands to the westward of the Pre-emption Line, were numbered at 7,000, while those residing on the Military Tract and the lands to its southward about the Chemung and Susquehanna, were estimated at 6,640. The people living in the principal villages then established were enumerated as follows: Canandaigua, 99; Geneva, 100; the Friends' settlement, 260; Culver's Town, at head of Seneca Lake, 70; Catharine's Town, 30; Newtown, now Elmira, 100; Chemung Town, three miles down the river from Newtown, 50.

THE DEVELOPMENT.

The Development of the region of the lakes followed rapidly upon the initial events of settlement. The advance of improvement was along the water-side, and nearly every point became the scene of enterprise. The ruins of limekilns, the marks of charcoal pits, the rock-cuts where saw-mills and still-houses dotted the streams, remain as mute reminders of the leading industries of the time. The woodman's axe was swung with telling effect in the early years, and as the clearings continually expanded in area, loggings, raisings and road-openings evoked the endeavors of the inhabitants, on many an enjoyable occasion of general assemblage.

Saw and grist-mills were manufactories soon established by the settlers, who until their construction, were obliged to whip-saw logs for lumber, and pound their grain in mortars hollowed from the tops of stumps, with pestles attached to spring-poles. The first gristmill in Western New York was built in 1789, two and one-half miles from the site of Penn Yan down Crooked Lake Outlet, by Richard Smith, James Parker and Abraham Dayton. In 1790, mills were erected at the head of Cayuga Lake and near Canandaigua Lake; in 1791, they were in operation about the Chemung; 1792, on the sites of Naples and Owego; 1793, at Bath, the site of Corning and near Ovid; in 1794, or previous thereto, at the head of Seneca Lake.

The Friends, that peculiar people from Rhode Island whose religious belief died with its members from the earth, in 1789 harvested the first wheat crop raised in Western New York, which was floured in the grist-mill erected by them that year. The settlement of the twenty-five pioneers of the sect, in 1787, was about one mile south of the site of Dresden, and its location was determined on because of the extensive water power that could there be utilized. The first framed house in what is now Yates county, was constructed on a farm of 1,000 acres, set apart for the use of the founder of the Friends, Jemima Wilkinson, who joined the colony with a large number of followers, in 1789.

The promoters of the Pulteney estate were the most active developers of the Genesee Lands. After the location of Bath, every inducement was held out to settlers, and for several years its markets ranked high in importance. What were known as arks, constructions some fifteen feet wide and seventy feet long, were there made as well as at other points on the Chemung and tributaries, in 1800, and loaded with wheat floated down the Susquehanna to sea-board marts, where they were taken apart and both the lumber and the grain readily sold. The rising waters of these rivers in early spring, bore southward on their currents immense rafts of timber, to be fashioned into ocean fleets at the ship-yards of Baltimore.

THE INDUSTRIES.

The Industries of the time of settlement were dependent largely upon the abundance of forest products, and with the clearing of the land, enterprises that had flourished at an earlier day waned in importance, until like the primitive log-cabins only the sites remained. As the timber disappeared saw-mills were abandoned, asheries were rendered useless, charcoal-pits were no longer located, and maple-sugar making became almost a thing of the past. Lime-burning and distilling were continued in small constructions and with rude appliances, until the many plants of the pioneers had given place to the fewer extensive establishments with modern machinery.

The asheries were aggregations of leach-tubs, where lye was obtained from wood-ashes gathered from settlers' hearths, and subsequently reduced by boiling to the substance known as potash, which after a process of calcining became the grayish powder called pearlash. Charcoal-pits contained usually about ten cords of wood, compactly placed on end around an open center in which the fire was kindled. About the pile earth was banked with vents near the ground, and constant watching was necessary during the eight to ten days required for combustion. The limekilns were circular enclosures of stone built into earth-banks convenient to the waterways, and their blackened, crumbling walls remain reminders of the past, on many of the points of the lakes.

Maple-sugar making in the olden days was an operation amid sylvan surroundings, whose charms mitigated the few irksome features incident to the undertaking. The thrift and abundance of the maples about the lakes had awakened even the interest of the soldiers, and attracting the attention of the settlers in turn, the sugar-tree was spared no matter how ruthless the onslaught upon other growths of the forest. When the buds appeared in late February, the sugar-bush became the scene of activity. Trees were tapped and kettles hung, and as the gathering of the sap progressed, ofttimes a "sugaring-off" would cause assemblage of a company for merriment at night, while bonfires lighted far into the lonely woods.

The still-house equipment was far from complicated, and the determining requisite of a location was a living stream of water as supply to the mash-vat, in which the crushed corn or rye was fermented. The furnace fixtures for boiling the mass were of plain construction, but the workmanship of the worm was generally elaborate. The spirit of the grain, which entered its spiral length as vapor, was condensed to liquid form before its issuance. This pure product of the still was in almost universal use, the decanter usually appearing on the mantel above the fire-place. On public occasions it flowed without stint, and no general improvement or private enterprise was attempted without a liberal supply.

THE ANTIQUITIES.

The Antiquities of Central New York belong not to the early days of occupancy by this race, nor yet to the barbaric ages of its predecessor, but arise from conditions of a time so shrouded by the past as to be beyond the ken of Indian tradition. When white men first began settlement, a chain of ancient fortifications appeared to extend from the lower end of Lake Ontario to the southwestward, all occupying commanding positions, and oftentimes large areas. They are supposed to be the work of that mysterious people, the Mound Builders. The French probably discovered and took possession of these constructions, as their arms are found above weapons of primitive years.

The site of a fortification near the foot of Owasco Lake, is now known as Fort Hill, and occupied by a modern cemetery. Long after its builders had abandoned the locality, it was the seat of a village of the Cayugas, named by them Osco. This was the birthplace of the noted Indian chief, Logan, who after the murder of his family by the whites, became from a friend, an implacable foe, and was killed in 1780. An ancient work on the east slope of Cayuga Lake near Aurora, embraced with its embankments about twenty acres upon a hill between two ravines. Traces of occupation in prehistoric times are observable about the foot of Seneca and Canandaigua Lakes, in trench enclosures and similar structures for defense.

A mound or fortification of an elliptical form, was found by the pioneers, located on the dividing ridge between Lakes Seneca and Cayuga, near the south line of the present town of Ovid. The embankment, broken in its course by openings probably used for entrances, was about three feet in height, with a base several feet in width, and enclosed nearly three acres of land, on which as well as the construction itself, great forest trees were growing in 1800. A settler soon afterwards built a house within the space, and in the course of subsequent excavations, the teeth and large bones of several skeletons, pieces of a coarse kind of pottery, ornamental pipes and other relics of like character were unearthed.

Along the Chemung near Elmira, clothed like the surroundings by a dense forest growth when discovered by the whites, the remains of a fortification are most advantageously located to resist attacks of enemies. On one side is the river, on the other a deep ravine, and in the rear extends an embankment two hundred feet in length, fourteen feet in width and over three feet in height. An earth-work on the summit of Bluff Point embraced several acres in its low ridges, which were some eight feet in width, and faced along the sides with flat stones. Circular mounds appear about Lakes Lamoka and Waneta, and on the intervale at the entrance to Havana Glen, may be traced with other artificial formations of earth, one of triangular form.

THE LANDMARKS.

The Landmarks of the lakes were towering trees and other well defined natural objects, or mystic spots memorial of the deeds of a departed race, which left euphonious names upon the waters and about their shores. The highlands overlooking Seneca Lake from the southward, were known as Ta-de-vigh-ro-no; Bluff Point, the promontory separating the east and west branches of Lake Keuka, as O-go-ya-ga; Bare Hill on Canandaigua Lake, the legendary place of origin of the Senecas, as Ge-nun-de-wah. The most distinguishing feature of the west shore of Cayuga Lake, retains the full significance of its fame as "The great waterfall of the woods," in its Indian appellation of Taughannock Falls.

The Big Tree under whose boughs the Indian treaty of 1797 occurred, was an immense elm that stood on the banks of the Genesee, visible for miles along the "pleasant valley," as the name of the river signifies. The traditionary elm at the head of Seneca Lake was some four feet in diameter at base, and bore its crest proudly above its fellows. It marked the southwest corner of the Military Tract, and later the division of Steuben and Tompkins counties on the north line of Chemung. In a storm of wind and rain, July 15th, 1890, this tree was laid prostrate, when its trunk was found to be a mere shell through decay of heart from great age. Gigantic elms and walnuts cast their shade over corn-growths of the intervales in Indian days.

The Painted Post at the confluence of the Tioga and Conhocton Rivers, was a noted landmark in the annals of settlement and in the history of Indian affairs long before. There are various traditions as to its origin, one stating that it marked the grave of Captain Montour, a son of Queen Catharine, and who there died of wounds received at the Battle of Newtown; another, that it was a monument of great antiquity, from time to time renewed, and originally erected to commemorate the death of some celebrated war-chief, whose name and deeds were long forgotten. The whites in after years placed an iron representation of a warrior on the spot, and in its stead, in 1894, reared a granite shaft crowned by the bronze figure of an Indian.

The Old Castle, the designation of the grounds near the site of Kanadaseaga where the Senecas laid their dead away, was covered by an Indian orchard, and the remains were undisturbed by the whites because of a stipulation to that effect made in the treaty of purchase. For many years at plowing time, warriors of the Iroquois came and watched this orchard to see that its sward remained unturned by the husbandman. This mystic spot alone of the numerous burial places of the aborigines about the lakes, was not subject to despoliation when found, though amid the leaf-strewn mounds in many a forest glade, the conquering race located the lone and mournful graves of the early years.

THE TRAVELERS.

The Travelers through Central New York at the time of settlement were attracted as are the thousands of tourists of the present day, by the charms of scenery, yet unsurpassed, but then in primeval beauty. Few chronicled their observations, but of that number all were favorably impressed. One journal of travel, written in February, 1792, contains the following entry: "On the evening of the third days' journey from Whitestown, we were very agreeably surprised to find ourselves on the east side of the Seneca Lake, perfectly open and free from ice as in the month of June. This after having passed from New York over a country completely frozen, was a sight pleasing and interesting."

A visitor to the lakes in the autumn of 1792, thus records of Cayuga and Seneca or Canadasega Lake, as it was then sometimes called: "Thirty-five miles from Onondaga Lake, I struck the Cayuga Lake. The road is tolerable for a new country, with but three houses upon it; the land excellent, and very heavy timbered. This lake is from thirty-five to forty miles long, about two miles wide, and abounds with fish. Twelve miles west of the Cayuga, with no inhabitant upon the road, is the Canadasega Lake, the handsomest piece of water I ever beheld. Upon a pretty slope stands a town called Geneva, which consists of about twenty log-houses, three or four frame buildings, and as many idle persons as can live in them."

Louis Philippe, King of the French from 1830 until his flight to England in 1848, where his death occurred two years later, during the ascendancy to power of Napoleon Bonaparte was a wanderer in America. In 1797, accompanied by his two younger brothers, he journeyed from Buffalo to Canandaigua and thence to Geneva. Sailing in the sloop over Seneca to Catharine's Town, the party walked to Newtown, and after a ten days' sojourn, proceeded down the Chemung and Susquehanna Rivers upon an ark. The royal visitors passed a night with Peter Pitts, a land-owner at the foot of Honeoye Lake; were entertained at Canandaigua by Thomas Morris; at Catharine's Town by George Mills, and at Newtown by Henry Tower and others.

Alexander Wilson, author of "American Ornithology," in the autumn of 1804, with two companions made a pedestrian trip to the lakes. The party proceeded from Philadelphia overland to the Susquehanna; thence up its course and that of the Chemung to Newtown; down Catharine Valley and the east shore of Seneca Lake to near Lodi, where they crossed over to Cayuga Lake, and taking skiff followed the waters to Lake Ontario. The author embodied his experiences in a poem entitled "The Foresters," and in the footnotes to that portion devoted to Seneca Lake scenery, mentioned the waterfalls, the towering walnuts, the eagles and snow-white storks, and the many impressions of marine shells in the rocks of the shore.

THE MILITIA.

The Militia of the State in the early days included all able-bodied citizens between the ages of eighteen and forty-five years, not exempt by law from military duty, and the training consequent upon the organization rendered it possible at all times for the government to call effective troops to its support should the exigency arise. The Constitution of 1777, ordained that a proper magazine of warlike stores, proportionate to the number of inhabitants, should be established in every county, but this provision was never fully carried out, although arsenals were located for each division of the militia and armories provided for each regiment.

The regiments were composed of eight companies, including one of artillery, which assembled for drill in their respective localities some three times a year. Thus every village was the scene of martial demonstrations, upon the expanse of green extending before the portals of the old-time taverns, and incidents of training days yet enter largely into their tales of tradition. Each militia-man was required to have his accoutrements in order, and as a general thing all took pride in possessing muskets which could be relied upon as exponents of good marksmanship. The members of a company of cavalry were invariably skillful riders, well-mounted on picked horses of mettle and endurance.

The ordnance furnished by the State to the artillery companies consisted generally of guns throwing a six-pound ball, and to-day these cannons may be found at the principal centers of population, mute reminders of by-gone evolutions of the field, save when their voices awaken the echoes on occasions of special or national celebration. In modern warfare these relics of the past would be of little avail, and probably will never again be required for use in army ranks. Several kegs of ammunition were furnished yearly by the government to each company for practice purposes, and in after ages, from many a clayey bank, once behind a target, rusty projectiles may be dug greatly to the interest of antiquarians.

General training was a gala day to the community, causing an assemblage of all from far and near, and awakening a feeling of fraternity by extending the general acquaintance of individuals. The companies of a regiment gathered on the occasion, each vying with the other in the completeness of equipment and the proficiency of drill. The officers in full regimentals presided over the military maneuvers, while the strains of martial music sounded and the cannon boomed, reminding the aged present, of Revolutionary days, and arousing in the youth in attendance, resolves to conserve the liberties then won. These events of patriotic import occurred annually in the autumn months, and continued until the close of 1845.

THE SCHOOLS.

The Schools of the settlements were early established and advanced with the development of the general system of the commonwealth. At the first meeting of the State Legislature in 1787, a law was passed providing for the appointment of the Regents of the University, and in 1789, certain portions of the public lands were appropriated for school and gospel purposes. In 1793, the Regents recommended the establishment of common schools, and two years later the first of the many laws for their encouragement went into effect. Prominent among the advocates of education at that time was Ezra L'Hommedieu of the State Senate, owner of a tract of land at the head of Seneca Lake.

The educational institutions of the county-seats of the lakes, were first established as follows: Canandaigua Academy, March 4th, 1795; Auburn Academy, February 14th, 1815; Ithaca Academy, March 24th, 1823; Ovid Academy, April 13th, 1826; Geneseo Academy, March 10th, 1827; Owego Academy,

April 16th, 1828; Penn Yan Academy, April 17th, 1828; Lyons Academy, March 29th, 1837; Elmira Academy, March 31st, 1840; Waterloo Academy, April 11th, 1842; Bath Union School, July 8th, 1846; Corning Union School, April 13th, 1859; Watkins Union School, April 3rd, 1863. Other early incorporations were: Cayuga Academy at Aurora, March 23rd, 1801; Geneva Academy, March 29th, 1813; Prattsburgh Academy, February 23rd, 1824; Skaneateles Academy, April 14th, 1829; Avon Academy, April 13th, 1836; Seneca Falls Academy, April 27th, 1837.

The denominational schools date from April 14th, 1820, when the Auburn Theological Seminary, a Presbyterian institution, was chartered. The Genesee Wesleyan Seminary at Lima, was established by the Methodists, April 30th, 1833, and merged in Genesee College February 27th, 1849. Hobart College at Geneva, in control of the Episcopals, on April 10th, 1852, succeeded Geneva College, chartered April 5th, 1824, in which was merged Geneva Academy.

Starkey Seminary on the west shore of Seneca Lake, was incorporated by the Christians, February 25th, 1848. The Elmira Female College was founded by the Presbyterians, April 13th, 1855. The charter of Cook Academy at Havana, was secured by the Baptists in August, 1872. The Free Baptists laid the corner-stone of Lake Keuka College, August 21st, 1888.

One Normal School is included in the seats of learning along the route of the Military Expedition—at Geneseo, chartered March 29th, 1867. Two colleges were incorporated, and extensive structures erected, which are now occupied by other institutions. The People's College was authorized, April 12th, 1853, and the New York State Agricultural College at Ovid, April 15th, 1853. The Cook Academy succeeded to the site of the former, and the Willard Asylum to the latter. Through the enterprise of Charles Cook, the People's College was located on a farm of two hundred acres at Havana, January 8th, 1857, but subsequent failure to fulfill statutory requirements resulted in a loss of the land-grant, which made possible the greatness of Cornell University.

THE INSTITUTIONS.

The Institutions established by the State in Central New York, are of the classes, educational, charitable and corrective, which evidence the cosmopolitan character and diversity of interests, to which the old domain of the Iroquois has attained. They were founded on liberal lines, and date from 1816, when the building of Auburn Prison was commenced. It was completed in 1819, at a cost of $300,000, exclusive of the labor of convicts. The last located about the lakes, was through act of June 26th, 1880, which was the initial event in the establishment of the Agricultural Experiment Station at Geneva.

Cornell University which overlooks Cayuga Lake at Ithaca, was chartered April 27th, 1865, through the enterprise of Ezra Cornell, but is more a monument of public than private liberality. In 1862, Congress passed an act granting to the States which should provide schools for the promotion of Agriculture and the mechanic arts, thirty thousand acres of public lands for each senator and representative. This fund was evidently intended to aid many establishments of New York, but the entire proceeds of the State's share, amounting to nine hundred and ninety thousand acres, became of benefit to the University, upon compliance with the conditions of the legislative enactment of incorporation.

The State Hospital for the Insane, located on the eastern shore of Seneca Lake at the site of the old New York State agricultural college and farm, ranks as the leading institution of its kind. It had its inception in an act passed April 8th, 1865, authorizing the establishment of the Willard Asylum for the Insane. An act to establish and maintain an institution for the relief of indigent and disabled soldiers and sailors of the State of New York, was passed June 3rd, 1872. Bath was chosen as the place of location of the Home; the buildings were commenced in 1878, and opened for the reception of inmates on Christmas day, 1879.

The New York State Reformatory at Elmira, commands from its wall-environed heights, a beautiful view of the valley-ways up which the troops of the Military Expedition marched in pursuit of the Iroquois. To the northward extends the vale down which the defeated warriors trailed, and to the southward, almost within the shadow of the buildings, rest the dead from the ranks of the Confederate prisoners, confined along the Chemung during the Civil War. The site was selected in pursuance of an act authorizing the appointment of commissioners to locate a State Penitentiary or Industrial Reformatory, passed April 29th, 1869.

THE RELIGION.

The Religion of the Iroquois taught the return of thanks for all bounties received from the Great Spirit, who in their worship was addressed by particular speakers, followed by feasting, and closing with dancing and other recreations. While prayer was offered, the dust of tobacco sprinkled on live coals of fire, arose as incense with the supplications. Their great religious festivals were held semi-annually, when the convocations were general, and the celebrations of thanksgiving continued from three to six days. With them, "The groves were God's first temples," and the budding leaf, the sprouting plant, the ripening grain had deepest significance of immortality.

The Jesuits at an early day founded missions in the villages of the Five Nations, having attained so extended a knowledge of the territory of the lakes as to map its main features in 1664, but the constant aggressions and unceasing wars of the whites, rendered of little avail the efforts of the missionaries to inculcate the doctrines of peace. Father Isaac Jogues, in 1642, was the pioneer priest in the Onondaga country, but he and many of the sixty as devoted souls, who in the succeeding hundred years labored to uphold the cross in the wilderness, met death at the hands of the Iroquois, who denominated members of the clergy as "black coats," when they came to regard them with distrust as agents of a rapacious race.

The preachers of the Protestant denominations in later years too often but prepared the way for the machinations of the speculators, who were known as "gamblers" among the despoiled denizens of the forest. In 1765, the Rev. Samuel Kirkland came on a mission to the Indians at Kanadaseaga, and was revered by them for his good works, yet as commissioner of the State of Massachusetts, he conducted the treaty of 1788, which was the beginning of the end of the land-titles of the Six Nations. It was not long after this event, that all the sects of civilization had representative congregations in the settlements, endeavoring to promote the welfare of community, and the societies then organized are still flourishing.

The vagaries of religious belief have had striking illustrations in Central New York, not however to prosper long at the places of inception. The Friends whose deeds about Lake Keuka Outlet are now ancient annals, had faith that Jemima Wilkinson was controlled by the Divine Spirit in propagating the tenet that celibacy was indispensable to a pure life. Mormon Hill near the north line of Ontario county, is the pretended place of discovery by Joseph Smith in 1827, of the golden plates of the Book of Mormon, and Brigham Young, after living for a time west of the head of Seneca Lake, resided long at Canandaigua. The Oneida Community, established by John H. Noyes in 1847, held all things in common up to 1879, when their peculiar family relations were abandoned.

THE FOLK-LORE.

The Folk-lore of the forest-environed homes was a natural result of lives, isolated and under the weird spell of the wilderness. Though the country of the lakes was new to the settlers, it was old in its traditions of a mysterious past. The race which had departed left no monuments to mark the period of its power, but the influence of its occupancy was over all, and thus under conducive conditions the superstitions of an older time, throve even more vigorously than in the lands from which they had been transplanted. Upon the border-land of barbarism and civilization, the characteristics of the past and present came in contact and commingled.

Mystic spots were many in the lore of the Iroquois, who would desert village sites if believing that evil influences were there dominant, and the localities thus under a ban were often regarded as eerie places by the whites. The Indians' observance of the phases of the moon; their forest signs governing seed-time of maize; their note of natural phenomena, and rare wood-craft, became lines of guidance with many of the pioneers. Thus survive still on the farmsteads, sayings that rain will fall when the dip of the crescent moon is such that the powder-horn of the hunter may be hung thereon while he rests from the chase, and corn-planting time is at hand when white-oak leaves resemble feet of squirrels in size of growth.

Witchcraft extended its enchantments over the dreamers of both races, and the silver bullet, like the charmed arrow, was prepared in secret for the were-wolf's heart. The spectres of the dead appeared alike to the Iroquois and the credulous settlers, and many a hill and hollow bore the prefix of "ghost," to its appellation in the olden days. Then also, in accordance with the folk-lore of the whites, occasionally occurred the curious custom of "Telling the bees," on the death of a member of the household. Those who observed the usage, tapped gently on each hive and whispered of the dead, in order that the little honeymakers might not forsake their abode, because of having to ascertain the fact themselves.

The superstition of the vampire, that horror of the grave which was supposed to harbor with the dead yet derive its sustenance from the living, had one illustration at least about Seneca Lake. Down the western shore not many miles from its head, in the early years the corpse of a young woman was exhumed, and the heart and other vital parts committed to the flames. The grewsome tale comports in a remarkable manner with the general sayings in regard to vampires. Of several sisters, all in succession had wasted away, until but one remained and she was ill. Though in the grave for many months, the burned portions of the body were fresh in appearance. The living sister, undoubtedly from mental relief, recovered her health after the event.

THE TREASURE.

The Treasure of the earth was an object of unceasing quest by many settlers of more adventurous spirit than their fellows, for few of the localities of the lakes were devoid of legends of lead and silver mines known to the Indians but undiscovered by the whites. This idea of unearthed ore of value was not confined to individuals, but engaged the thoughts of entire communities, and even extended its influence to the halls of legislation, for in many of the early sales of land the gold and silver mines were reserved by the State. This provision indicative of wide-spread belief in mining possibilities, dated from Colonial days, and was a feature of all patents then granted.

The lead-mine mystery appears to have been given greater credence than other tales of treasure-trove, for from the shores of Ontario to the banks of the Chemung and Susquehanna, the rock-walled tributaries of the lakes and rivers were explored by the pioneers intent on finding the mystically-marked boulders, that were said to bar the entrances to caverns rich with deposits of metal. Indian lore located treasure at an elbow of a stream of Seneca Lake, and settlers regarded the tradition worthy of consideration, as at angles of ravines rock-fissures most abound; but all search for mines westward of Oneida Lake have been unavailing, while to the eastward veins of ore appear from the Hudson to the Mohawk, the Delaware to the St. Lawrence.

The Iroquois in roving bands visited at intervals their old-time haunts, for many years after the remnant of their race had been assigned to reservations. Silently and unexpectedly to the pioneers they came, as spirits of the past, and tarried but a brief period along the waters before departure. No cabin home, lone in the woodland depths, was molested on these occasions, and no reason could be conjectured for such visitations, save to obtain a portion of the treasure, forever hidden by forest-craft from the whites. There are authentic statements to the effect that settlers who had granted favors to the Indians were taken to their rendezvous, but in the dead of night and by so devious a route they could not find the way by day.

Long after the last Iroquois had left his ancestral trails, the quest continued, and to-day those versed in wood-lore may trace in many a vale, the thicket-over-grown excavations or note upon the shore-skirting cliffs the drill-indentations of the fortune hunters. Geologists have pronounced against the probability of finding lead and silver ores in paying quantities in the region of the lakes, but out-croppings are known to exist, and what the revelations of the future will be none may say. The secrets of the rocks are not ascertained by cursory examinations; only exhaustive investigations will disclose their treasure, which is evidenced in as great degree at present as was the great salt bed beneath the lakes a score of years ago.

THE SALT-SPRINGS.

The Salt-springs were found throughout the State as settlement progressed; the brine varying in degree of saturation, from the 70° of the outflow at Onondaga to the brackish waters known as "deer licks." The existence of these springs and others of a mineral nature now famous for their medicinal qualities, was known to the Indians, and in most cases only discovered through chance by the whites. Their locations were not willingly revealed by the discomfited race, and doubtless brine springs yet remain unknown. The facts are well authenticated, that the Iroquois would borrow kettles of the settlers about the heads of Seneca and Cayuga Lakes, and return them filled with salt.

The journal of Father Lallemant, who visited the region in 1645, makes the first mention in history of the salt springs of Onondaga Lake. Their value was ascertained during the Colonial period; in the treaty with the Six Nations they were to be jointly used by the whites and Indians forever, and the State reserved for salt purposes the territory surrounding. The first salt there produced by settlers, was made in 1789, by Asa Danforth and Comfort Tyler in a kettle suspended from a pole upheld by crotched sticks. The first caldron kettle with arch, was used by James Van Vleck in 1793, and solar works were constructed in 1821. The manufacture of salt was begun to the northward of Cayuga Lake in 1798, and later at other points in Western New York.

The boring of wells on the sites of springs of weak brine in the hopes of increasing the supply and saturation, was commenced at an early date, but with the tools of the time, the depths attained hardly exceeded two hundred feet, and the efforts generally ended in disappointment. After the discovery of the petroleum deposits of Pennsylvania in 1859, drilling was resumed in this State, but in search of oil. With the improved appliances it was possible to sink wells more than one thousand feet within the earth, and thus the salt field of Central and Western New York was discovered. Many of the borings of this period are either valuable wells of mineral water, or costly exponents of failure termed "dry holes."

The Lake Country of which Seneca is the geographical center, in its limits is nearly conterminous with the salt tract of the State. From westward of the Genesee, eastward to the section south of Oneida Lake, the drills after passing through the rocks of shale and limestone, have penetrated deeply into rock-salt. This bed is now known to be the source of the springs of Onondaga; its northern boundary appearing to be about on a line with the foot of the lakes, while its extent to the southward is not defined. In its central portion it lies less than fifteen hundred feet below tide.

The works of the Glen Salt Company, one mile down the west shore of Seneca Lake, were completed in 1894, the last of twenty-five blocks of the field established since 1880.

THE ROCKS.

The Rocks of Western New York, with the exception of the saline deposit, contain mineral wealth neither of great value nor extensive dissemination. The rock-formations preclude the existence of the precious metals as well as the baser ores. These include all the strata lying between the primary rocks and the coal measures of Pennsylvania, which dip toward the south and overlie each other on a general level from west to east, though bent, far in the distance of the latter direction. The strata are distinguished mainly by the fossils which they contain, and vary in thickness from a few inches to many feet.

The whole country from the shores of Ontario to the altitude of the Alleghanies, rises in a series of terraces, bounded at their northern edges by the out-croppings of the principal rock groups. Through these terraces the beds of the lakes have been riven, which renders the slopes about their outlets of level aspect, while hills that approach in elevation the heights of mountains, encompass their heads. Lake Ontario in its whole width from the Genesee River northward, is excavated in the lower part of the Medina Sandstone, the Oneida Conglomerate and Gray Sandstone, and the Hudson River Group. Its waters from a surface of 232 feet above tide, extend to a depth of 368 feet below sea-level.

The Hudson River Group that limits the depth of bed of Ontario, is above the Utica Slate; and the Trenton and Black River Limestones, the Calciferous Sandrock and the Potsdam Sandstone, lead down to the Granite and Gneiss of the primary rocks. The Medina Sandstone forms the bluffs of the southern shore of Lake Ontario, and from this formation upwards and southward, the rocks consist principally of a series of limestones, shales and sandstones, each passing into the other by gradation, or with the line of separation distinctly marked. The geographical appellations of those points where the members of a rock-group display greatest development, were adopted as their geological designations.

The shores of Seneca from their central location and north and south extension, well present the record of the rocks. The formations in their order from Ontario to the foot of the lake are the Medina Sandstone, the Clinton and the Niagara Groups, and the Onondaga Salt Group. The Corniferous Limestone and Marcellus Shale have out-croppings of fifty feet each, along the Seneca; and above, the Hamilton Group extends for hundreds of feet. Ten feet of Tully Limestone separates the Hamilton shales from the Genesee Slate, 150 feet in thickness. Then ensues the Portage Group for 1,000 feet, and above it, the Chemung Group rises in the rock-ribbed hills, to the Old Red Sandstone and the Conglomerate of the Carboniferous system.

THE STREAMS.

The Streams mingle with the currents of the lakes, either through watercourses of alluvial banks or ravines that cut deep into the rock-walls of the shores. The inlet and the outlet waters generally flow gently through valley and plain, and over gravelly beds, but the outflows of Lakes Keuka and Skaneateles are through rocky channels; the former in its descent to Seneca, a distance of seven miles, falling 270 feet, and the latter descending 250 feet in five miles. Seneca River is the main drainage stream of the Lake Country, receiving its waters from Canandaigua eastward to Oneida Lake, where it assumes the name of Oswego River.

The streams coursing from the height of land, southward to the Chemung and Susquehanna, invariably rise in upland vales between the heads of the lakes, and at an elevation of hundreds of feet above their surface waters. Lakelets are frequently the feeders of these watercourses, which in their channels, nowhere show a rocky bed in flow from source to river. This is in substantiation of the theory, that the lake-beds of Central New York are in true rock-fissures of the earth, resulting from some great convulsion of the past, which not only rent asunder the vast crevasses of the valleys, but caused as well the secondary rifts of the uplands.

The lakes receive many tributaries from the uplands, which from hill-environed springs wind through quiet dales, to foam through rapids and over cascades in rock-walled courses as they near the end. Should the stream thread an old-time rock-fissure in the latter part of its flow, the wearing action of its waters during the ages past, has formed a glen of curve and pool and tranquil reach. Such are the characteristics of Watkins and Havana Glens. Streams which have wrought their own channels, course through gorges, not deep but broad and with angles and abrupt turns, as do Big Stream and Hector Falls Creek on Seneca, and Fall and Taughannock Creeks on Cayuga.

The waterfalls of the streams are numerous, and form the most picturesque features of the landscapes of the lakes. In the course from upland to valley, the water-flow encountering rocks of different degrees of hardness, has worn them irregularly, the soft shales forming a declining surface, while the compact strata have retained their forms. To this action is due the fact, that the locations of the waterfalls are either at the face of the cliffs or worn deeply into the bluffs. Hector and Montour Falls on Seneca, and Fall Creek Falls on Cayuga, are illustrations of the former condition, while the latter is evidenced by Lodi and Glenora Falls on Seneca Lake, and Taughannock Falls on Cayuga Lake.

THE WATER-WAYS.

The Water-ways were the avenues along which coursed the tide of civilization, and vantage grounds that had been well-chosen as places of occupancy by the Iroquois, were appropriated without question by the settlers. The streams which from their forest shrouded sources perennially flowed, turned many mills on sites now silent, or marked by quiet hamlets. Where commercial advantages aided the growth of towns, their upbuilding was gradual in most instances, but with some the efforts of great landowners effected a speedy development, while others after flourishing for a time, fell slowly into inevitable decadence.

This waning prosperity was the natural result of changed conditions, principally the exhaustion of forest resources. Great centers of enterprise are only possible at considerable distances from each other, and in the settlement of a country the final supremacy in the case of rival towns rests on the fact of more favorable location. On the outlet of Lakes Lamoka and Waneta, midway between the heads of Lakes Keuka and Seneca, in 1793, Frederick Bartles of New Jersey, laid out a village, which he named Frederick Town. He built saw and grist mills, and in May, 1798, 100,000 feet of boards were floated from this point to Baltimore, an evidence of the immense volume of business there transacted while lasted woodland products.

The idea that the site of Watkins was to be the location of a place of commercial importance, because at the head of Seneca Lake, was doubtless entertained by John W. Watkins, who began improvements soon after his great land purchase, and also an expectation of Samuel Watkins, as in no other town in Western New York are the streets located with greater regularity or with more metropolitan features of length and breadth. The village now includes what was known as Savoy, founded on the western slope of Seneca by Isaac Q. Leake, and three miles down the eastern shore of the lake, at Hector Falls, John B. and Samuel S. Seeley once conducted a thriving business, having grist and fulling mills, a still-house and a foundry, an inn and store, of which foundation stones alone remain.

It was an era when water carriage was the only available means of moving the vast bulk of commodity of a section of diversified products, continually expanding in area of cultivation. The trend of commercial currents, at first exclusively to the southward, was turned eastward as well, by the improvements which resulted in the connection of the Mohawk and Oswego River systems by canal, in 1796. The flow in the latter direction was augmented by the opening of the Erie Canal in 1825; the Cayuga and Seneca Canal in 1828, and the Crooked Lake and Chemung Canals in 1833. One scheme was never realized— the building of a ship canal from the lakes to Sodus Bay, along the shores of which a city was platted in the early days.

THE STEAMBOATS.

The Steamboats first appeared upon the waters of the Lake Country during the '20's, but incorporated companies were concerned in navigation affairs on but three of the lakes, Cayuga, Seneca and Keuka. There were no olden-day organizations to build steamboats on Canandaigua, Skaneateles or the smaller lakes, but vessels propelled by steam early ploughed their waves. For many years after settlement, sailing craft were numerous as freighters. A sloop was launched on Seneca at Geneva, as early as 1796, to run as a packet to the head of the lake, and a schooner began trading trips on Lake Keuka shortly after 1800.

The Cayuga Steam Boat Company, of which David Woodcock was President and Oliver Phelps, James Pumpelly, James Benjamin and Lewis Tooker, Directors, built at Ithaca the steamboat "Enterprise," which made her first trip on June 7th, 1820. One hundred and fifty passengers were aboard, and it took from 10 a. m. till 6 p. m. to reach Cayuga Bridge, where a great concourse of people, martial music and the roar of cannon greeted the arrival. Elijah H. Goodwin was in command. The Cayuga Lake and Inlet Steamboat Company was incorporated February 25th, 1828, with a capital of $20,000. Headquarters were at Ithaca, and the Directors were Francis A. Bloodgood, Richard V. DeWitt, Elijah H. Goodwin,

Alvah Beebe and S. DeWitt Bloodgood. The Seneca Lake Steamboat Company was formed by legislative enactment, April 6th, 1825. Its incorporators were Samuel Watkins, Henry Dwight, Samuel Colt, Joseph Fellows, James Rees, Nicholas Ayrault and associates. Headquarters were at Geneva, and the capital stock $20,000. The first steamboat on Seneca Lake, the "Seneca Chief," began running three years after this event, but its proprietors were J. B. and R. Rumney. The boat first landed at the head of the lake, July 4th, 1828, amid the shouts of a multitude, volleys of musketry and the boom of cannon. Captain E. Miner was in command, and it had required over five hours' time to make the distance from Geneva.

The Crooked Lake Steamboat Company with a capital stock of $5,000, and headquarters at Bath, was organized April 18th, 1826, by Dugald Cameron, John Magee, William Hastings, Samuel S. Ellsworth and Abraham Wagener. It is not known however, that through this organization was built the first steamboat of Lake Keuka, which was known as the "Keuka," and in the year 1837 plied between Hammondsport and Penn Yan, with Joseph Lewis as Captain. The first steamboat of Canandaigua Lake was launched at its foot in 1827. It was in command of Isaac Parrish, and called the "Lady of the Lake." Skaneateles Lake was first sailed by a steamboat in 1831; the "Independence," commanded by Captain Wells.

THE FERRIES.

The Ferries of the lakes were established some score of years after the initiatory enterprises of the kind, at Cayuga Lake Outlet and at the Genesee River. The former was the first ferry in Central New York, and run under the proprietorship of John Harris, the pioneer of that locality, while the latter was located soon afterwards, yet in 1789, by Gilbert R. Berry, an early settler on the river to the west of the site of Avon. After the finding of the low-water fords and before the construction of bridges, ferries came into general use upon the streams, many of which were navigable to the light craft of the times, and in consequence declared by legislative enactment to be public highways.

The valley lakes of Owasco, Skaneateles, Canandaigua and Crooked or Keuka, as it is known at present, are narrow in their courses like Seneca and Cayuga, but of less than half as great lengths, and to this configuration is doubtless due the fact that but one of them, Lake Keuka, was ever crossed by a ferry chartered by the State. The route connected the eastern and western shores, and touched at the southern extremity of Bluff Point, at one time the site of quite a village. April 21st, 1818, Isaac Kingsbury was authorized to maintain the ferry; March 22nd, 1828, Hiram Gleason secured the charter for ten years, and April 12th, 1838, Francis Correll was granted a continuance for a similar term, the limit of the legal life of the privilege.

The first ferry of Seneca Lake was maintained by John Goodwin, where the North Hector ferry ran till 1897. His charter extended for ten years from April 4th, 1820, but on April 17th, 1826, John Starkey was granted the route for fifteen years. May 2nd, 1845, Ira Fowler and Alfred Goodwin were authorized to continue this ferry for a similar term. April 15th, 1825, John Maynard, Ethan Watrous and William Howard were empowered to conduct a ferry for twenty years, from "Lancaster village in the county of Seneca to Dresden village in the county of Yates." April 3rd, 1829, Terah Carter acquired the right to keep a ferry for fifteen years, from Big Stream to Peach Orchard Point. At an early day, Miles Raplee and Charles Goff ran an unchartered ferry across the lake at Lodi Landing.

The ferries of Cayuga Lake, other than those over outlet waters, date from April 17th, 1816, when was established the ferry, which for fourteen years from April 15th, 1825, was continued by James Kidder, Amos Goodwin, Matthew N. Tillotson and David Ogden, and for the same length of time from April 5th, 1844, by Ira Almy and Horace C.

Tracy. January 21st, 1826, James and Jacob Carr were authorized to keep a ferry at Union Springs; May 18th, 1836, Stephen Mosher for twelve years; December 14th, 1847, John Carr for ten years; April 5th, 1853, Thomas Patten for ten years. February 25th, 1828, Samuel Griggs, Asa Foote and Ebenezer Goff were granted a ferry charter at Griggsport. April 24th, 1829, John McLallen acquired ferry privileges at Frog Point, but May 20th, 1836, William Carman was accorded the rights, which by renewals were extended to 1885.

THE CANALS.

The Canals, which in after years linked the lakes with the waters of adjacent rivers, were projected soon after settlement was well advanced, and until completion their establishment was ably advocated. The Western Inland Navigation Company was incorporated March 30th, 1792, with power to improve the channel of the Mohawk River and build canals to Lake Ontario and Seneca

Lake. The work was begun at Little Falls in 1793, and three years later boats passed through to Oneida Lake. The company gave up its rights west of that point in 1808, and in 1820, sold out to the State for $152,718.52.

The Erie Canal was commenced at Rome July 4th, 1817, and finished in October, 1825, at a cost of $7,143,789.86. As then constructed, it was 363 miles long, forty feet wide at top, twenty-eight at bottom, and four feet deep. The completion of the work was celebrated by civic and military demonstrations from the lakes to the sea, and at New York City the ceremonies were especially imposing, the day of the arrival of the first boat over its course, bearing Governor Clinton and other officials of the State. As this craft entered the canal at Buffalo, October 26th, the event was heralded by cannon arranged along the line, and in an hour and twenty minutes the signal passed to New York.

The Cayuga and Seneca Canal for about half its course is formed by slackwater navigation upon the Seneca River.

The descent from Geneva, its western, to Montezuma, its eastern terminus, is seventy-four feet. The Seneca Lock Navigation Company was incorporated April 6th, 1813, for the purpose of improving the outlet of Seneca and Cayuga Lakes, and the Cayuga and Seneca Canal Company was chartered April 20th, 1815. Its capital was increased to $60,000 in 1816, and again augmented the following year. The proposition for assuming the work by the State was approved in 1825, and the interest of the company purchased for $33,867.18. The canal was completed in 1828, at a cost of $214,000.

The Crooked Lake Canal and the Chemung Canal were abandoned by the State in 1877 and '78. The former was begun in 1830, and finished in 1833. It had a descent of 269 feet from Lake Keuka to Seneca Lake, by twenty-seven locks. The construction of the Chemung Canal was commenced in 1829, and it was completed in 1833, at a cost of $344,000. It connected Seneca Lake with the Chemung River at Elmira, and its feeder was navigable from Horseheads to Corning. On both canal and feeder were fifty-three locks with an aggregate rise of 516 feet. By the junction Canal, a private enterprise, it was connected with the Pennsylvania Canal. The Chenango Canal and the Genesee Valley Canal were also abandoned in 1878.

THE LAND-ROUTES.

The Land-routes at the commencement of pioneer undertakings followed the trails of the Iroquois, who so well had chosen their pathways along the waters and over the divides, that many of the thoroughfares of to-day yet follow their winding courses. They were invariably of easy grade, and in the patches of primeval woods that remain along the lake-shores, these ancient ways, worn by the noiseless tread of feet encased in moccasins, may still be traced. The troops in command of General Sullivan were led by guides of the Oneida Nation over Indian trails, made by the axe-men, of sufficient

THE LAKE COUNTRY. 123

width for the passage of the artillery.

Two public highways to the lakes were commenced in 1791, which became important routes for immigration. One was built from Oxford on the Chenango River, to the head of Cayuga Lake, and the other from Whitestown on the Mohawk River, to the foot of Seneca Lake. This was known as the Geneva Road, and the old army track continued it as a thoroughfare to the Genesee River, from which point only an Indian trail extended to Niagara. The water-courses encountered in the opening of these lines of travel were crossed at fording places, with the exception of ferriage at the foot of Cayuga Lake, while over the marshy places stretched the log track-ways known as corduroy roads.

The Cayuga Bridge, the most extensive work connected with the land-routes, was considered one of the greatest public improvements in the State, and for a time regarded as the dividing line between the East and the West. The company for its construction was incorporated in 1797, and consisted of John

Harris, Thomas Morris, Wilhelmus Mynderse, Charles Williamson and Joseph Annin. The structure spanned the foot of Cayuga Lake, and was one mile and eight rods long, twenty-two feet wide and the same number of feet between trestles. It was finished September 4th, 1800, having required eighteen months for completion at a cost of $150,000. The bridge fell in 1808, was rebuilt in 1813, and abandoned in 1857.

Turnpike Roads extended in 1810, through Owego, Newtown and Bath to the Genesee River, along the courses of the Susquehanna and Chemung; through Ithaca, Catharine's Town and Bath, toward Lake Erie; over the Geneva Road to the Genesee, thence to the mouth of Buffalo Creek; from Oneida Lake, by the site of Rochester to Fort Niagara. Highways connected these turnpikes from Owego to Ithaca and Cayuga; from Newtown to Catharine's Town and Geneva; from Bath to Penn Yan, Friends' Settlement and Geneva; from Bath to Naples, Canandaigua and Sodus Bay. Over these thoroughfares, which are yet main routes of travel, lines of stages were established to flourish until superseded by the railways.

THE STAGE-LINES.

The Stage-lines were important factors in the affairs of the central section of the State, during the first quarter of the present century. Everywhere by lake and stream were they established, linking homes and hamlets with the main towns, and extending mail facilities to remote settlements. Though at first confined to the turnpike roads, and like the toll-gates distinctive features of those highways, stage-coaches soon began to thread all thoroughfares connecting the larger villages, which as head-quarters of their daily operations, became centers of marked business activities; the winding of the drivers' horns announcing the arrivals on the scene, as do the whistles of the locomotives of to-day.

The first location of stage-lines by law in the Lake Country was on March 31st, 1804, when the legislature granted to Levi Stephens and Jason Parker the sole right of running stages from Utica to Canandaigua, for the term of seven years. Trips were required to be made twice each week from May to October; then the travel demanded three every week, and finally daily runs. April 6th, 1807, John Metcalf was given similar privileges for the same length of time, between Canandaigua and Buffalo. Stages however, were running from Canandaigua and Geneva to Albany as early as 1797, when a weekly post was established; mails having been extended from Canajoharie to Utica in 1793, the inhabitants on the route providing for the expense.

The villages south of the lakes as well as those to the northward became great stage-line centers, each vying with the others in the efforts to reach outside points by this mode of conveyance. The stage-coaches on the main roads were gaily caparisoned but ponderous affairs weighing upwards of a ton, each drawn by four horses sure-footed and strong. The teams were changed at frequent intervals, and kept in fine condition by especial care. A dozen passengers with light baggage were carried even over the rough roadways of the hill-courses. The arrivals and departures were enlivening events of a place, occurring at stated hours with much bustle and exhilaration as accompaniments, for true time was a requisite to the good repute of the route.

The inns of olden days were located at such short distances apart, that travelers could find entertainment at almost any point where night overtook them. Many of the settlers thus denominated their log-houses, and those who did not observed the custom of leaving the latch-string out to wayfarers who were in need of their hospitality. The taverns succeeded the inns, but differed from them in being of more substantial and commodious structure, and many are yet in use either as dwellings or public houses. The bar was a main equipment, and while passengers were unrestrained by law in their thirsty proclivities, an act was passed in April, 1817, prohibiting stage companies from employing drivers who were addicted to drunkenness.

THE RAILWAYS.

The Railways were projected along the water-courses of Central New York at an early date. The Mohawk and Hudson, the first line to be constructed in the State, was chartered in 1826, and opened to traffic in 1831. An act to incorporate the Ithaca and Owego Railroad Company was passed in January, 1828, and the road was opened in April, 1834. These initial railways were closely connected with the fortunes of the Lake Country; the former having become the first link in the chain of the New York Central lines, and the latter ultimately becoming part of the Lackawanna system.

Two lines of railway traversed New York State from east to west, at the close of 1851, one passing south and the other north of the lakes, and known respectively as the "Erie" and the "Central" roads. The New York and Erie Railroad Company was formed in July, 1833, but reorganized in 1835. The act authorizing the road was passed in April, 1832, and the preliminary survey of the route was made the same year by DeWitt Clinton, Jr., the final survey by Benjamin Wright, occurring in 1834. The line was opened from Piermont to Goshen in September, 1841; to Binghamton in December, 1848; to Elmira in October, 1849, and to Dunkirk in May, 1851.

The New York Central and Hudson River Railroad Company was formed November 1st, 1869, by the combination of the two lines of railway mentioned in title. The "Central" Company was organized under an act of April, 1853, authorizing the consolidation of the railroads between Albany and Buffalo. These numbered ten, ranging in date of construction from 1831, up to 1853, when the direct line from Syracuse to Rochester was completed. The railroad from Syracuse to Auburn was finished in 1836; Auburn to Rochester in 1840, and Rochester to Buffalo in 1852. The Hudson River Railroad was chartered in May, 1846, and opened its entire length in October, 1851.

The lines of railroad operated by the Northern Central Railway Company, were constructed through the Lake Country in 1851. The Fall Brook route, which went into operation in 1877, is the outgrowth of the mining interests of the Fall Brook Coal Company, organized in 1859. The Delaware, Lackawanna and Western Railroad Company, the lessee of many routes of railway in Central New York, completed its double-track line to Buffalo in 1882. The Lehigh Valley Railway Company is the result of the consolidation of several railroad organizations in June, 1890, when its double-track road was built. Other lines of the lakes are not of independent management.

THE PRESS.

The Press of Central New York was early established, but the subject of newspaper endeavor throughout its extent, if properly presented would require a volume in itself, and only the pioneer publications may be mentioned in these sketches. In every center of population about the lakes to-day, are well supported and ably conducted journals, which in their columns advocate the interests of community and make faithful record of the locality, and while far in advance of the standard of excellence of their antecedents in the field, no less credit is due the periodicals of the olden days.

Previous to 1800 newspapers were published in Steuben, Ontario and Cayuga counties, but in Tioga, the fourth county of the lakes at that time, one was not issued till that year, when The American Constellation was started at Union Village. The Bath Gazette and Genesee Advertiser, the first paper of Western New York, was established in 1796 at Bath, by William Kersey and James Eddie. The Ontario Gazette and Genesee Advertiser was commenced at Geneva, by Lucius Carey in 1797, but two years later removed to Canandaigua. The Levana Gazette was issued by R. Delano in 1798, and two other papers of Cayuga county appeared in 1799; the Western Luminary and the Aurora Gazette.

The towns having more than one newspaper in addition to those enumerated, founded during the first quarter of the century were as follows: Auburn—Cayuga Patriot, 1814; Advocate of the People, 1816; Cayuga Republican, 1819. Geneva—Impartial American, 1800; Expositor, 1806; Palladium, 1816. Waterloo—Seneca Farmer, 1822; Republican, 1822; Observer, 1824. Elmira—Telegraph, 1816; Investigator, 1820; Republican, 1820. Binghamton—Broome Co. Patriot, 1812; Republican Herald, 1818; Republican, 1822. Canandaigua—Ontario Freeman, 1803; Republican, 1824. Bath—Steuben Patriot, 1815; Farmers' Gazette, 1816. Ithaca—Seneca Republican, 1815; Republican Chronicle, 1820. Penn Yan—Herald, 1818; Yates Co. Republican, 1824. Lyons—Republican, 1821, issued six months; Advertiser, 1822.

Other initial publications of the lakes were: The American Farmer, Owego, 1810; The Cayuga Tocsin, Union Springs, 1812; The Seneca Patriot, Ovid, 1815; Genesee Farmer, Moscow, 1817; Palmyra Register, 1817; Livingston Journal, Geneseo, 1822; The Lake Light,

Trumansburg, 1827; The Tioga Patriot, Havana, 1828; Seneca Falls Journal, 1829; Newark Republican, 1829; Clyde Standard, 1830; Vienna Republican, Phelps, 1831; Naples Free Press, 1832; The Corning and Blossburg Advocate, Corning, 1840; The Chemung Democrat, Jefferson now Watkins, county-seat of Schuyler, 1842.

THE SLOOPS.

The Sloops and schooners of the olden days no longer plough the waters of Central New York. The lakes which bore hundreds of sailing craft engaged in the commercial transactions of the pioneers, now save for pleasure purposes bear not one upon their bosoms. In that early time nearly every owner of a point was also the proprietor of a sail-boat, in which was taken marketward the products of the field and forest, and off more than one cove of the shore molder yet the skeletons of settlers, who were swept from the deck to death by the swinging boom of a sail.

The Sloop of the Seneca launched at Geneva in 1796, amid a great public demonstration, was the pioneer packet-boat of the lakes. The craft was of forty-tons burden, and made trips to Catharine's Town, later known as Havana and now called Montour Falls. From the head of the lake this landing was reached by a sail up the curving course of the Inlet through Catharine Marsh, and the distance between Geneva and Catharine's Town being some forty miles, gave rise to the old-time saying that Seneca Lake was of that length. The surveyors with Sullivan's troops recorded the measurement of the route along the east shore of the lake, as thirty-six miles.

A schooner known as the "Lyre of Tioga" and hailing from Catharine's Town, was the central figure in a memorable event in the annals of Seneca. In 1825 by legislative enactment, the Inlet in its portion through Catharine Marsh was declared to be a public highway. Through interests at the head of the lake however, a draw-bridge was constructed over the stream, which was deemed of too narrow build for the purposes of navigation, by the people of Catharine's Town. Accordingly they placed a cannon loaded with broken andirons, on the schooner's prow, and sailing down the Inlet waters tore the bridge to pieces by its discharge.

A New York paper of date of November 17th, 1823, under the heading "Inland Navigation," thus mentioned a noted Seneca Lake schooner: "Arrived yesterday from the town of Hector, Tompkins county, the schooner 'Mary and Hannah' of Factory Falls, Captain Jackson commanding. This is the first vessel which has reached the port of New York through the western canal. She brings a cargo consisting of 800 bushels of wheat, three tons of butter and four barrels of beans, all of excellent quality." Factory Falls was the designation of the site of old-time industry, now known as Hector Falls and distinguished only for its picturesque cascade.

THE FRUITS.

The Fruits of fall ripen nowhere in greater perfection than throughout the Lake Country. Orchards there bear with the greatest abundance, and vineyards yield products of the finest flavor. Grapes have been cultivated for upwards of half a century, the first vines being planted during the '40's, and the shores of one lake having but little precedence over the others. The slopes of Lakes Keuka, Canandaigua and Seneca seem to be peculiarly adapted to the growth of vineyard products, while not as great success has been attained along Cayuga Lake or the bodies of water to the eastward.

The first grapes at the head of Lake Keuka were planted by Rev. William Bostwick, who did not raise them to sell however, and the first shipments were from a vineyard grown from cuttings from his vines, by William Hastings in 1847. It was the same year, 1847, that a Mr. McKay set out two acres of grapes on Canandaigua Lake. The first vineyard located on Seneca Lake, as near as can be ascertained, was on lands belonging to Isaac Hildreth, at Big Stream in 1845. From these beginnings the industry has assumed vast proportions, much of the acreage being on soil stony and steep and once considered of little value for agricultural purposes.

The fruits of the lakes are not wholly of modern culture, for the Iroquois had extensive orchards of apples, peaches and plums, which were ruthlessly laid low by troops of the Military Expedition. The wide-spread destruction attendant on that event, may be inferred from the statement of one journal, that on the east side of Cayuga Lake alone, no less than 1,500 peach, besides apple and other fruit trees were felled to the ground. This was upwards of a century ago, and a century previous to that march of havoc, in 1665, a chronicler had declared the region of the lakes of Central New York, "Capable of bearing all the fruits of Provence and Touraine."

The settlers obtained fruit from Indian apple-trees that had been overlooked by the troops or from sprouts of the original stumps, until the orchards planted by themselves came into bearing. These clumps of trees may be seen on many of the homesteads of the lakes, generally occupying a gravelly knoll, with a pile of stones at the side, marking the chimney-site of the log-cabin that once stood upon the spot. Natural fruit was the product of these orchards, and it was worth but little save to manufacture into cider. This was done by mashing the apples between two upright corrugated timbers operated by a sweep, and known in early days as "nut mills."

THE TOPICS.

The Topics of the foregoing pages are neither treated at length nor in attempt at exhaustive consideration. Each subject could be amplified, but the intent of the work is rather of a cyclopedic character than an extended narration of the past. In gathering the facts presented, gazetteers, session laws, local histories, newspaper files and old residents' recollections have been consulted. There are many themes of interest in the Lake

Country not touched upon at all, because their initial events were of later date than the pioneer period. Notably is this true of the Glens, which have become world-wide in fame as tourist-resorts. Their openings to the public have been of comparatively recent date, though along their banks in olden days, o'er ways that may still be threaded by those versed in wood-lore, in Indian file through countless years there trailed a race, whose deeds about the lakes have become in greater part, "But a memory and a recollection."

THE LAND OF GOLD.

BY
JOHN CORBETT.

THE SKETCHES.

Alaska as the place of sojourn during the months of May and June, 1898, gave opportunity for the observations that are embodied in the following sketches of the Land of Gold. In that far-away realm life-lines are plain and primitive, and from the civilization of the crowning years of the century the transition was to the crude conditions of pioneer days. The trip was made after a week of leisure in New York and a month of sight-seeing about Seattle; both busy marts of commerce, whose ships sail out over the seas to meet where the Orient becomes the Occident. Imbued with the spirit of settlement scenes by life in Central New York, existence in Alaskan wilds was of interest to The Writer and his partner, E. L. Becker, also a native of the Lake Country.

THE LAND OF GOLD.

SKETCHES OF A SOJOURN ALONG ALASKAN SHORES.

The Land of Gold is one of vast extent and immense resources; though its river currents are of great velocity, its mountain heights unconquerable, and its frozen wastes nearly interminable. The forest wealth of this domain of almost immeasurable distances, will prove a source of profit to generations yet to be. The mineral deposits will not be exhausted while ages elapse, for should the time ever come when the gold no longer glints in the miner's pan, then will the ores of lesser worth demand and receive attention. The waters of the coast-line teem with fish and fowl, whose progeny in future will augment the world's food supply; while on the grass of the foot-hills where now feed the moose and sheep, the flocks and herds of civilization will find sustenance. The soil of the southern shore of Alaska supports a wonderful woodland growth, and where cleared for cultivation yields quick-maturing crops in abundance. The mold suitable for plant life is deep and fertile, and only awaits the hand of the husbandman to bring forth all hardy grains and fruits in their season. Alaska is an empire in area of physical features, and unlimited in its possibilities of industrial and commercial development.

THE SHIP.

The Ship sailed from Seattle, as fell the shades of evening of an April day. To the eastward and the westward, the Cascades and the Olympics from their snowy heights, yet glinted the glories of the sunset. Above, the sky was cloudless, and beneath, the surface of the Sound was tranquil as a lakelet. For four days the sail was up the inland passage, behind islands which shut off the swell of the sea, except at Hecate Strait and Dixon Entrance, where open waters were encountered. Through wide reaches and narrow channels the steamer held its way; wooded heights on either hand, and evidence of life of fish and fowl everywhere. Indian villages with their totem poles and peculiar places of burial were passed, and now and then a vessel would be met. This portion of the trip was as if through a new world, and all on board were exhilarated by the entrancing scenes. One quiet day inland, the ship sailed out of Sumner Strait, and as night fell was rolling in the swells of the Pacific. May day found it still in the open ocean, and visions of flowery fields mocked the memory during the misty hours that ensued, before the boat was gliding through the tranquil waters of Cook Inlet.

The Inlet is fifty by two hundred

miles in extent, with waters that soon lose their deep-sea tint through shoaling, and the vexing of the submerged sands by adverse currents. Snow-capped mountain chains marked by glaciers and volcanic peaks, guard its timbered shores. The ship rode at anchor at its head waiting for the turn of the tide, in the midst of wonderland; bathed by the sun in beauties indescribable, as it sank into a cloudland sea of gold behind banks of pearl. To the east and west were snowy mountain ranges, far beyond the wooded forelands; to the south extended open water with the skyline barely discernible; to the north rose Mt. Sushitna, its summit clothed in eternal snows, a mile in height above sea-level. The northeast tributary of Cook Inlet is known as Turnagain Arm, and up its narrow course the tide surges with great velocity, rising to the height of thirty feet. On the flow, the vessel held her way at morning, going with the turbid flood over quaking shallows and treacherous sands, to an anchorage at the mouth of a mountain stream, where at the ebb it was beached, precisely as the exploring ship of Captain Cook made landing along its waters in 1778.

THE CAMP.

The Camp was in the shelter of mountains, rising thousands of feet above the waters of the stream that skirted the plain on which it stood. The configuration of its location was such that the tints of the dawn long lighted up the environing peaks at morning, and this distinguishment established its appellation of "Sunrise." Its low-eaved cabins of logs among the stumps and shrubs of a hastily completed clearing, were pioneer constructions in every detail save the old-time fire-places of stone. The door-ways broad and inviting, opened into hospitable though rudely furnished interiors where benches served as chairs and boxes frequently as tables, but where food was plentiful, plain and nourishing. On the outskirts of the settlement were reared the white tents of the new-comers—the "tenderfeet," who perhaps were getting an experience of frontier life for the first time in their existence. From the plain the wooded slopes swelled on either side to timber-line, and above the snow-fields rose to towering heights, while in the foreground the valley of the stream wound from the tidal flats of Turnagain Arm, far into the interior of the uplands.

The laws of a camp are few yet effective, and aim to secure the inviolability of the person and property. So long as a member respects the rights of others, he may be a law unto himself on moral lines. A life for a life is the rule in a mining community, and a thief is sometimes given short shrift before the rope's end. More often however, a meeting is called, and the offender is escorted by a committee to the next camp, who herald there his guilt. His course thenceforward to the courts of civilization, is a succession of custodial trips by committees to camps, with his wrong-doing ever proclaimed at their termination. The law's delay has no exemplification among men of the wilderness, who generally can be grouped as to their motives for seeking solitude, under three gradations. There are those who love treasure-hunting for itself, and are ever at the frontier in the quest for gold. Others before financial failure have enjoyed the fruits of success, and hope amid new scenes to retrieve their fortunes. Lastly are the men of mystery, who in lonely lives are endeavoring to expiate acts of the past, and somewhere through the years by the homestead hearths, hearts may be waiting and breaking for the absent ones.

THE CLAIM.

The Claim where the quest is made for gold, if on placer ground has an area of twenty acres. In the Sunrise district the local laws allow the staking of the location in rectangular form, and hence it is usual to extend the claim up the stream some fifteen hundred feet, with a width on either hand from its center of about three hundred feet. The ground is first prospected by the miner, who with pan and pick and pack of camp-kit has threaded his way far up some lonely gorge. He seeks an unexplored region, for if anyone has preceded him to the spot his labors may be in vain. A claim however, that has not been developed within the time prescribed by mining law, reverts to the public and may be relocated. After prospecting the placer-site, stakes marking its bounds should be set within ten days, and before the expiration of the time of thirty days, a record must be made at the office of the district. The assessment work required to perfect the title and ensure permanent possession, must equal yearly the value of one hundred dollars, but the miner not only has the remainder of the year of location but all of the next one, in which to complete his first development.

The trails lead to the lonely claims, following the waterways and extending in many instances but as courses marked by lines of blazed trees. Yet up these pathways the miner packs his belongings, if he make permanent camp upon his claim. With the pan he labors if alone, patiently washing the sands and carefully hoarding the yellow grains when found. With what is termed a rocker much more effective work may be done, a larger amount of soil be handled and greater treasure obtained. If sluicing be the method employed, the boxes must first be made, and oftentimes from lumber manufactured from trees upon the site by the slow and laborious process of whip-sawing. With these crude appliances the treasure-seekers toil on, their lives brightened only by the glint of gold they are trying to secure. Away from all home ties with only simple food rudely prepared, a bed of boughs and a blanket for nightly rest, they diligently delve, but they have the best of health, the clearest air and purest water, the grandest of mountain scenery, a summer-tide without a night, their personal liberty to its fullest extent; an existence free from the cark of worldly affairs, and almost ideal in its isolation.

THE GOLD.

The Gold of Alaska shows its traces everywhere throughout the soil, but aside from the pay-streak the flakes are very small and widely disseminated. Where tides rise high along its glacial beaches, where streams foam over boulder-beds, where mountains rear snowy heights, the golden grains may be found. Yet it is tons of earth to ounces of gold in the main, and the individual miner may expend years of effort without achieving a competence. Capital and co-operation are required to wrest the treasure from its fastnesses, for whether in veins of quartz or placer deposits the gold is deep in its affinity to bed-rock. Nature nowhere has her treasure-house easy of access, in that realm of rugged physical characteristics and forbidding climatic conditions. Beneath the evergreens generally of giant growth, the underbrush thrives thickly, and in placer ground this forest wealth must be cleared away, if operations would extend beyond the bed of the torrent that roars through its boulder-strewn course down the mountain gorge. The moss and mold which hide the surface of the slopes below timber-line, give place to snow and ice above, and render prospecting for quartz lodes an undertaking fraught with difficulties, such as even old miners hesitate to encounter.

The mining of gold in general is conducted on too limited a scale to compass satisfactory results. The precious metal is plentiful, and in time modern machinery moved at the behest of financial interests will accomplish at a profit what is now impossible for efforts of the individual. The Treadwell mine with its thousand stamps in operation pays dividends on a valuation of millions, but a miner with pestle and mortar on its free-milling yet low-grade ore could scarcely earn his salt. The quest for gold is as old as the annals of mankind, yet the details of the process of the separation of its grains from the soil through the use of water, are the same as when in barbaric days its glint first gave suggestion of its worth. The crude constructions of the placer grounds cannot retain all the value of the sands that are washed within them, and for ages the waste has continued for the wealth of ancient days was thus secured. The thirst for treasure has transformed lives, as when once the pursuit is engaged in the search for the elusive substance seldom ceases, and in the endeavor to wrest fortune from the reluctant earth it appears as if the greatest obstacles had to be surmounted where gold most abounds.

THE SCENE.

The Scene of these sketches is a land where night has no terrors from the darkness. No twilight falls at eventide, no stars appear in summertime even at the midnight hour, and the dawn is only known to be at hand through sunlight gleam on mountain tops afar. The season for placer mining extends from early June until late September, and on the extensively worked claims men are employed on day and night shifts, no artificial light whatever being required for the latter. In this realm of lofty and snow-clad mountain ranges, the grandeur of the rising and the setting of the sun is indescribable, the light flashing from crest to crest of billowing peaks at morning, and fading one by one from the view at evening. The mountains are unique in their magnificence, and rising abruptly from sea-level the full impressiveness of their heights is realized. About their bases the forest clings; spruce and fir and birch clothing the slopes to timber-line, a distance of perhaps a thousand feet. The grasses extend their sward and the mosses creep above, and then the eternal snows. The reverberations of thunder are never heard among the peaks, but ever and anon a sullen boom sounds down the gorges, the accompaniment of the tremor of an earthquake.

The clime about Cook Inlet is not inhospitable even during the winter months. The snow falls deeply but the mercury sinks not much below twenty degrees, a temperature that is bearable in an atmosphere of great dryness and so clear that objects scores of miles away appear as if just up the valley. During rain-fall it is as if a mist prevailed; there are no down-pours and electric storms are unknown. In early May sleeping in a tent, rolled in a blanket upon frozen ground, was attended with no discomfort, but in camp or cabin during the hours of night at all seasons warm coverings are a necessity, and to insure health and physical comfort woolen garments should be continually worn. The miners as a rule are men of fine physique and great endurance, a result largely due to their natural mode of life in surroundings conducive to bodily well-being. Miners are in one sense machines whose wasted energies require replenishment with hearty articles of diet, such as whole-wheat flour, coffee, bacon and beans, which form the staple food of the camp. Their arduous work or tramps over the trail give requisite exercise; they breathe airs uncontaminated by the effluvia of civilization, and as a consequence disease and depression are virtually unknown.

THE SHORE.

The Shore of Alaska was skirted for the entire distance from Sunrise to Seattle, on the return voyage. Stops were made at Tyonik, Snug Harbor, Homer, Saldovia, Orca, Natchek, Yakutat, Sitka,

Juneau and Ft. Wrangel. Tyonik now principally an Indian settlement, was a town of importance when the Russians were endeavoring to colonize about Cook Inlet. In the rocky bluffs at the entrance to Snug Harbor the sea-gulls nest, and myriads appeared to be in the air, on the clefts of the cliffs and about the waters. Salmon which agreeably replenished the ship's larder were taken off the sand-spit at Homer, and at Saldovia the anchor was cast for a three days' sojourn before transference to the second boat of the trip. The resonance of bells from a Greek Church chapel floated on the air one evening, the first time such sound had been heard in months. It was a sweet concordance over the quiet waters which were aglow with beauty as the sun went down, bringing into view nearly one hundred miles to the northwestward, the volcanoes Iliamna and Redoubt with the smoke-banners of their internal fires floating above their snowy crests. Rounding Cape Elizabeth, the course was continued along the shores of Kenia Peninsula to Prince William Sound.

The mists hung low over the waters, which is characteristic of the Sound the sailors say. The first stop was at a copper mine, at the base of a cliff a thousand feet in height; at Orca an immense salmon cannery was a feature of interest, and at Natchek the sails were furled while a storm raged on the Pacific. Through the Gulf of Alaska the sighting of whales was a frequent occurrence, and before anchoring at Yakutat the course for sixty miles was along the Malaspina Glacier, which extends its icy waste from the coast nearly to Mt. St. Elias, the corner-post of Alaska. In the island-studded harbor of Sitka the ship tarried for a while, and in the finest Greek Church of America Sunday services were witnessed, most of the worshipers being Indians. This is a restful spot where life to the unambitious should be a calm content. Through tide-fretted straits and tranquil sounds where eagles hold unmolested sway along the shores, the sail was made to Juneau, a town extending over foot-hills shadowed by rocky heights with the Treadwell mine across the waters, and all accompaniments of civilization save the telegraph. Three days of sight-seeing, and the third ship of the trip was boarded for the inland passage to Puget Sound. As if over summer seas the vessel sailed, touching at Ft. Wrangel and other ports amid most charming scenes.

THE RACE.

The Race that in time to come may dominate Alaskan shores, is the race that has held its own though one nation has come and gone, and another is now overrunning the land but remaining no longer than to secure its mineral wealth. The Indian of Alaska is a patient personage. The forms of Russian altars are before him, but he still erects his totem pole and reveres the rites of his pagan ancestry. His cabin though of logs has its central-fire on a pebbly bed with a smoke-hole in the roof above, precisely as did the bark-abodes of his race in days of yore. The skins of moose or bear cover the ground about the fire-bed, and squatted amid her half-clad offspring the woman of the household performs her simple duties. Thus are the domiciles of the older inhabitants, but in the habitations of the younger members of the tribe may be found some of the articles of civilization. There is no order of location in the construction of the dwelling-places. Over knolls and through dales they are erected wherever the fancy of the owners dictate, but the general extension of the village is governed by the trend of the shore of land-locked bay or mountain stream, whose waters from their snowy source are life-giving in their purity.

A canoe race across the waters of the strait was an event in the celebration of Independence day at Juneau. The graceful craft were fashioned from the trunks of giant firs, and each contained nearly a score of Indians, all young men of notable athletic appearance. The paddles dipped, the blades rising and falling with the regularity of the sweep of wings when wild-fowl fly, and over the waves like black swans on their course glided the contesting canoes. It was a demonstration of vigor, training and determination, that evidenced its participants were far from the period of race-decadence—the opinion generally entertained of the aborigines. A "potlatch" was another interesting feature that came under observation. It was given by an Indian as a preliminary to the erection of a totem pole, and invitations to members of his tribe were made by a harangue from a canoe as it was paddled by their habitations along the water-front. A series of dances and feasts followed until all had been entertained, the festivities beginning at the evening hour with the principal partakers bedecked by paint and trappings. Old usages long prevail with any people, and time which will obliterate barbaric customs will also sweep away the stunting superstitions, that retard advance of civilization.

www.ingramcontent.com/pod-product-compliance
Lightning Source LLC
Chambersburg PA
CBHW030259170426
43202CB00009B/812